Ready Steady Cook

The Top 100 recipes from your favourite TV chefs

Digital food photography by Steve Lee

This book is based on the television series *Ready Steady Cook* produced for
BBC Television by Endemol UK Productions.
Executive Producer: Linda Clifford
Series Producer: Pauline Doidge
Commissioning Executive for the BBC: Dominic Vallely

Published by BBC Books, BBC Worldwide Ltd
Woodlands
80 Wood Lane
London W12 0TT

This edition produced for
The Book People Ltd,
Hall Wood Avenue, Haydock, St. Helens WA11 9UL

First published 2003
Text © Copyright Endemol UK Plc 2003
The moral rights of the authors have been asserted
Food photography by Steve Lee © Copyright BBC Worldwide 2003

ISBN: 0 563 48729 1

Commissioning Editor: Vivien Bowler
Project Editor: Helena Caldon
Copy-Editor: Mari Roberts
Cover Art Director: Pene Parker
Design Manager: Sarah Ponder
Designer/Photo Art Director: Lisa Pettibone
Home Economist: Joss Herd
Stylist: Lucy Pearse
Production Controller: Arlene Alexander

Set in Caecilia and Foundry Sans
Printed and bound in Italy by L.E.G.O. spa
Colour separations by Radstock Reproductions Ltd

Ready Steady Cook

The Top 100 recipes from your favourite TV chefs

Compiled and edited by Orla Broderick

With recipes from

Ross Burden
Ainsley Harriott
James Martin
Nick Nairn
Paul Rankin
Tony Tobin
Brian Turner
Phil Vickery
Lesley Waters
Kevin Woodford
Antony Worrall Thompson

TED SMART

Contents

Introduction

Presenting *Ready Steady Cook* is like a dream come true. From the very first time I opened my carrier bag of ingredients – it contained an aubergine, a couple of beef tomatoes and a packet of mozzarella cheese – I have felt totally at ease. Cooking has always been my passion. I seldom get stressed about it and cooking for friends gives me enormous pleasure. Entertaining and educating others in the process is even better. Perhaps that's why I enjoy presenting and cooking on RSC.

When I was first approached to take part in a new programme called RSC nearly nine years ago I knew we were on to a winner. Using a bag of surprise ingredients, two chefs would create a dish in twenty minutes while talking about it. This was my idea of a great show. My only reservation was whether chefs who had great reputations would be prepared to put themselves on the line, cooking their food while knowing they could lose to the other chef. Soon after a dry run in my own kitchen at home in South London the real filming took place in a studio with all the bright lights, cameras and a real live audience. I had been asked to make the pilot with Brian Turner, one of the country's top chefs with a fabulous reputation, so I was a tad nervous. Fortunately the pilot was a huge success with the BBC bosses and the programme went ahead. Now a red tomato and a green pepper will always be linked for me with RSC.

Working on the show is like being part of a great big happy family. It feels as if we're cooking in the kitchen with friends ... and then a few extra friends pop in for supper! A great deal of this good feeling is down to the lovely Fern Britton. She created the perfect atmosphere for the chefs to express themselves and whip up some amazing meals. And, boy, did we express ourselves. (None more so than Phil Vickery. He and Fern are now married.) She enabled us to show the viewers how easy cooking with fresh ingredients could be and how quickly it could be done.

Meeting people all round the country I get asked the same questions: surely the chefs really do know what's in the bag? Surely it takes longer to cook than twenty minutes? The answer to both is no. From the second that I say the words 'Ready Steady Cook', the clock starts counting down and the chefs blaze into action. There is always such an atmosphere as the guests turn out their carrier bags and the chefs decide there and then what dish or dishes they are going to make. I think that's why the show has retained its energy and freshness. There is always a surprise against the clock.

The chefs are not always pleased with their ingredients, however. Offal and squid get sniffed at, desserts sometimes get a thumbs-down and the odd exotic ingredient can confuse us all, but the results are always interesting. When the chefs are happy with their bag there can be much excitement. Three-course meals are created right before our eyes and presented in so many different ways. And all the chefs really want to win.

The occasions when things go wrong are always remembered, though. We all know about liquidizers with an attitude, especially when AWT's about, and I've got the stained shirts to prove it. Burnt fingers happen in the presence of Kevin Woodford and Brian Turner (whom most people think are brothers!). They just love to use the ovens and when I'm rushing from one side of the kitchen to the other it's easy to forget which pan or tray has been where until – ouch! And although we're up against the clock, half of them still don't know how to use the microwave. All the chefs do certain things under pressure. Lesley Walters kicks her leg in the air and calls everyone darling, Ross Burden becomes a geography teacher, James Martin creates a sugar basket, Nick Nairn makes a broth from anything and Kevin loves tossing salt all over the place (later, when I'm changing, I find it in the strangest of places). AWT makes a fried egg sandwich or, if he's got fifteen seconds, an omelette, Brian Turner does yet another impression of me ('What's he like?'), Phil Vickery gets 'philosophical', Tony Tobin delivers his funny one-liners and Paul Rankin becomes even more laid-back. He's good for the craic!

With all this knowledge it's hardly surprising that we've created thousands of recipes and in doing so have inspired many of you to get into the kitchen. In this new big *Ready Steady Cook* book we've selected favourite recipes from all the chefs, tried and tested for your pleasure and waiting to be recreated for your next lunch, dinner, supper, snack or tea party. I'm sure you will enjoy it as much as we all do, so let's get cooking!

Ainsley Harriott

Who's Who

Ross Burden

Ross Burden has been a feature on British screens for ten years. The model-turned-presenter has appeared on many shows around the world.

Ross is a trained naturalist and keen traveller; a degree in Zoology and an upbringing on the New Zealand coast have equipped him to explore the natural world for *National Geographic* and *Network of the World*. But he is best known for being adept in the kitchen on shows such as *Masterchef* and *Ready Steady Cook*. He has also filmed a healthy eating video with Joan Collins and has made five series for Taste. Ross has published the book *Food for all Seasons*, has written for the *Sun* and currently writes columns for two magazines.

Ainsley Harriott

Ainsley Harriott has participated on *Ready Steady Cook* as a chef since its pilot version, and is now the presenter of the programme. He first appeared on our screens as the resident chef on BBC1's *Good Morning with Anne and Nick*. Since then he has gone from strength to strength, winning the *BBC Good Food Magazine* award for Favourite Television Personality in both 1997 and 1998. Ainsley has several highly acclaimed BBC series to his name and has written numerous cookery books, including *Meals in Minutes*, *Low Fat Meals in Minutes*, *Ainsley's Barbecue Bible*, *Big Cook Out*, *Gourmet Express* and *Gourmet Express 2*. His latest book, *All New Meals in Minutes*, was published in 2003.

James Martin

James Martin opened the Hotel du Vin in Winchester as Head Chef aged 21. He is a regular on *Ready Steady Cook* and *Celebrity Ready Steady Cook* and is the resident chef on *Housecall*, BBC 1's successful daytime show. He is also a regular presenter on UK Food's *Good Food Live*. He has written a regular recipe column for *Ideal Home* magazine and his first book was *Eating In with James Martin*. His first series for UK Food was linked to his second book *Delicious!* and he has just finished a second series *James Martin: Sweet*. His third book, *Great British Dinners* will be published in 2003. He is the consultant to P & O on the restaurants and menus for their new ship *Ocean Village* and co-owns Underwood and James, a kitchen design/manufacturing company in St Albans.

Nick Nairn

A self–taught cook, Nick Nairn is a champion of fresh Scottish ingredients. He has a successful television career with regular appearances on *Ready Steady Cook*, as well as three previous series of his own with the BBC - *Wild Harvest*, *Wild Harvest 2* and *Island Harvest* – all with accompanying books. His most recent best selling titles are *Nick Nairn's Top 100 Salmon Recipes* and *New Scottish Cookery*, released in 2002. He also contributes a weekly column to the *Sunday Herald* and owns a highly successful cookery school near Stirling.

Paul Rankin

A regular on *Ready Steady Cook*, Paul Rankin also has a successful restaurant and business in his native Belfast, which he runs with his wife and fellow chef, Jeanne.

Paul and Jeanne worked together at Le Gavroche, the Roux brothers' restaurant in London. There they learned some of the tricks of the trade before working in Canada and California. On their return to Belfast they set up Cayenne, an award-winning restaurant with an informal feel. In addition Paul and Jeanne have four cafés, all supplied by their own bakery, as well as a neighbourhood restaurant called Rain City.

Paul has appeared with Jeanne in many TV programmes, including *The Rankin Challenge* and three series of *Gourmet Ireland*. They have published two successful *Gourmet Ireland* books and their new book, *New Irish Cookery*, was published in 2003.

Tony Tobin

Tony started cooking professionally at the age of 14 when he worked in the kitchens of a pub/restaurant in Warwickshire. After two years at Stratford-upon-Avon Catering College he worked in a succession of top restaurants and Tony is now the owner of the Dining Room in Reigate, Surrey.

Tony has appeared regularly on *Saturday Kitchen*, *Ready Steady Cook*, *Can't Cook, Won't Cook*, and presented *The Green Gourmet* for Carlton Food Network. He has also made guest appearances on numerous television programmes including *Food and Drink* and *This Morning*.

Ten of Tony's recipes appeared in the *Hot Chefs* book and his recipes are also featured in the *Big Ready Steady Cookbook* and *The Twelve Chefs of Christmas*. Tony is currently working on his first book, *Dressed For Dinner*.

Brian Turner CBE

Brian Turner trained at some of the most prestigious hotels and restaurants in Europe earning himself a prized Michelin star, which he held for ten years, before he opened his own restaurant Turner's, in Walton Street, Knightsbridge. In February 2002 Turner opened the Brian Turner Restaurant at The Crowne Plaza Hotel in Birmingham's NEC. His new stand-alone London restaurant Brian Turner Mayfair was launched at the Millennium Hotel London Mayfair in April 2003.

Turner has appeared regularly on *Ready Steady Cook*, and on *Food and Drink* and has also been a judge on *Masterchef*. He featured as resident chef for many years on *This Morning* before hosting his own series, *Out to Lunch* and *A Yorkshire Pudding* and *Anything you can Cook* for BBC.

In the Queen's Birthday Honours in 2002, Turner was awarded a CBE for his services to tourism and training in the catering industry.

Phil Vickery

Phil was born in Folkestone, Kent, trained in the Lake District, then went on to Gravetye Manor in West Sussex, followed by a short stint at Ian McAndrew's Restaurant 74 in Canterbury, and nine years at the Castle Hotel in Taunton.

Phil Vickery is a winner of the British Meat 'Chef of the Year' award, his other professional accolades include earning a Michelin Star for four successive years, winning the Egon Ronay 'Dessert of the Year' category, and having his restaurant named *Times* 'Restaurant of the Year'.

Phil Vickery has worked on *This Morning*, *Ready Steady Cook* and *Masterchef*, as well as *Phil Vickery's Pudding Club* – his own recent TV series for Anglia.

Phil's first book *Just Food* was published to great acclaim, and Phil has just finished writing his second, *The Proof of the Pudding*; He also writes a regular Sunday newspaper column and monthly features for leading food and women's magazines.

Lesley Waters

Lesley Waters trained and worked as a chef and trained other would-be chefs at Prue Leith's School of Cookery and Wine. She has worked in television since 1989, but in addition to *GMTV* and *Bazaar*, her work has included writing and presenting a series of network *Cookery Club* programmes for Chrysalis TV, appearing as resident cook for the Lifestyle Channel and for UK Living. She also co-presented a series for Anglia called *Bodyworks*, was one of the major presenters of *Can't Cook, Won't Cook* and is a *Ready Steady Cook* regular. Lesley also co-presented *Surprise Chefs* for Meridian and has guested on *Food & Drink*, *Celebrity Ready Steady Cook*, *Light Lunch* and the BBC daytime show *Who'll Do The Pudding*. She has recorded three of her own series for Carlton Food Network, *Real Food*, *Flavours from Abroad* and *First Taste*.

Lesley has written numerous books, her most recent publications being *Juice Up Your Energy Levels* and *New To Cooking*.

Kevin Woodford

After graduating with a higher degree in Management Studies, Kevin pursued a career as Assistant Principal in a college of Higher Education, during which time he first hit our television screens as a regular contributor on ITV's *This Morning*. These appearances were followed by roles as presenter of *The Reluctant Cook*, team member of *Ready Steady Cook* and a main presenter of *Can't Cook, Won't Cook* which was voted Best Daytime Show at The National Television Awards.

Outside of the numerous cookery shows, Kevin has presented the *Holiday* programme and co-presented its seasonal counterpart *Summer Holiday*. These programmes spawned a series called *Fasten your Seatbelt*, for which he received critical acclaim and he has also appeared as host of BBC1's *The Heaven and Earth Show*.

Kevin has written seven cookery books and he is a regular contributor to many leading magazines.

Antony Worrall Thompson

Antony Worrall Thompson has worked in many top restaurants and owns Notting Grill in Holland Park.

In 1998 Antony became resident chef for BBC2's *Food & Drink*. He is a *Ready Steady Cook* regular and presents *Saturday Kitchen*. He has also filmed several series for Carlton Food Network including *Worrall Thompson Cooks*, *Simply Antony* and *So You Think You Can't Cook*. He has guested on many programmes, including *This Morning*, GMTV and *Masterchef* as well as *Have I Got News For You*, *Shooting Stars*, *The Kumars at No. 42* and more. He was a team captain on BBC Radio 4's *Question of Taste* with Oz Clarke and a participant of *I'm A Celebrity, Get Me Out Of Here!* Antony has written numerous books, most recently the *Top 100 Recipes from Food & Drink*, and has contributed columns for the *Sunday Times* and *Daily Express*. He currently writes for *The Express on Sunday Magazine* and for Saturday's *Express*.

1 Parma Ham with Caramelized Balsamic Onion and Beetroot

PAUL RANKIN'S STARTER

Serves 2

2 tbsp olive oil, for frying

1 small red onion, thinly sliced

2 tsp light muscovado sugar

1 tbsp balsamic vinegar

4 cooked whole baby beetroot, halved

½ tsp Dijon mustard

1 tsp white wine vinegar

85 ml/3 fl oz extra virgin olive oil

50 g/2 oz rocket, watercress and baby spinach salad leaves (from a bag)

6 slices Parma ham, torn

salt and freshly ground black pepper

Some marriages seem made in heaven – this one certainly does. I love the saltiness of the Parma ham, which sets off the sweetness of the beetroot, while the salad provides a welcome peppery crunch. Each flavour is strong enough to balance the other yet still remain distinct. To do the Parma ham justice make sure you take it out of the fridge and allow it to come back up to room temperature before serving it.

1 Heat a small frying pan over a low heat and add the two tablespoons of oil. Tip in the onion and cook for 2–3 minutes until softened but not coloured, stirring occasionally. Sprinkle over the sugar and cook for a minute or so to melt, stirring. Pour in the balsamic vinegar and allow to bubble down, then tip in the beetroot and cook for a couple of minutes until heated through and caramelized, tossing the pan occasionally.

2 To make the vinaigrette, place the mustard in a screw-topped jar with the white wine vinegar and seasoning. Shake to dissolve, then add the oil and shake again until emulsified. Place the salad leaves in a bowl and pour over enough dressing to coat. Arrange the Parma ham with the lightly dressed salad leaves on two serving plates. Scatter over the caramelized beetroot and onion and serve.

2 Crab Bites with Mango Salsa

AINSLEY HARRIOTT'S
STARTER

Serves 4

2 thick slices white bread, crusts removed (about 115 g/ 4 oz in total)

175 g/6 oz can white crabmeat, drained

1 egg yolk

2 tbsp mixed chopped fresh coriander and flat-leaf parsley

4 spring onions, finely shredded

1 large mild red chilli, seeded and finely chopped

1 small ripe mango, peeled, stoned and diced

juice of 1 large lime

sunflower oil, for shallow-frying

salt and freshly ground black pepper

lightly dressed spinach, rocket and watercress salad, to serve

Shallow-fry these crab bites, as below, or for a healthier option bake them: lightly dust your hands with cornflour, shape the crab mixture into twelve even-sized patties and arrange, well spaced, on a non-stick baking sheet. Lightly spray with oil and bake in a preheated oven at 200°C/400°F/Gas 6 (fan oven 180°C from cold), for 10–12 minutes, turning halfway through, until crisp golden brown.

1 Place the bread in a shallow dish, cover with water and leave to soak for about 10 seconds, then squeeze out the excess water. Place in a food processor and add the crabmeat, egg yolk, coriander and parsley, and half the spring onions and chilli. Season to taste and pulse until just blended.

2 To make the mango salsa, place the mango in a bowl and add the remaining spring onions and chilli. Stir in the lime juice and season to taste. Set aside at room temperature to allow the flavours to develop.

3 Heat a frying pan with about 5 mm/¼ in of oil and shallow-fry twelve equal-sized spoonfuls of the mixture for 2–3 minutes on each side until puffed up and golden brown – you may have to do this in batches depending on the size of your pan. Drain on kitchen paper. Arrange the crab cakes on serving plates with the mango salsa. Add a small mound of the spinach, rocket and watercress salad and serve at once.

3 Thai Salmon Cakes with Dipping Sauce

NICK NAIRN'S STARTER

Serves 2

600 g/1 lb 5 oz salmon fillet, skinned and cubed

1 lemongrass stalk, outer leaves removed, finely chopped

50 g/2 oz bunch of fresh coriander, roughly chopped, plus extra sprigs to garnish

2 green chillies, seeded and chopped

3 tbsp Thai fish sauce (*nam pla*)

2 limes

1 garlic clove, crushed

1 tsp sugar

sunflower oil, for shallow-frying

about 2 tbsp plain flour

These wonderfully aromatic salmon cakes worked so well on the show that I often find myself making them at home. The addition of the lemongrass and loads of coriander, stalks and all, make them really fragrant. Serve with the dipping sauce, close your eyes and you could be on a street in Bangkok.

1 Place the salmon in a food processor with the lemongrass, coriander, chillies and one tablespoon of the Thai fish sauce. Grate in the rind from one of the limes and blitz in short bursts until you have achieved a smooth paste. Transfer to a bowl, cover with clingfilm and chill for at least 10 minutes (or up to an hour if time allows).

2 To make the dipping sauce, cut the lime that you have grated the rind from in half and squeeze one tablespoon of the juice into a small bowl. Add the remaining two tablespoons of the Thai fish sauce along with the garlic and sugar.

3 Heat a frying pan with about 5 mm/¼ in of oil. Divide the mixture into twelve portions, then using slightly wetted hands roll each into a ball. Gently press down each ball to flatten slightly and form a patty. Tip the flour on to a plate and dip in each patty, shaking off any excess.

4 Fry the salmon cakes in batches for 1–2 minutes on each side until tender and lightly browned. Drain on kitchen paper and arrange on warmed square serving plates. Place a small bowl of the dipping sauce to one side and cut the remaining lime into wedges and use as a garnish with the coriander sprigs. Serve at once.

4 Chilli Squid with Mango Salad

TONY TOBIN'S STARTER

Serves 2

sunflower oil, for deep-frying

50 g/2 oz plain flour

1 tsp ground cayenne pepper

pinch of salt

200 g/7 oz squid (about 3 small tubes), cleaned and cut into rings

FOR THE SALAD:

1 firm ripe mango, peeled, stoned and flesh cut into julienne

6 baby spring onions, halved and shredded lengthways

2 garlic cloves, crushed

2 tsp toasted sesame seeds

3 limes, peeled and cut into segments

1 tbsp mixed chopped fresh coriander and mint

This dish has everything going for it – an excellent combination of flavours and textures and it looks fab to boot! The mango salad is extremely easy to prepare and keeps happily at room temperature for a couple of hours. Take care when deep-frying: hot oil should never be left unattended.

1 Preheat a deep-fat fryer or a deep-sided pan one-third full of sunflower oil to 190°C/375°F. To prepare the salad, place the mango in a bowl and add the spring onions, garlic, sesame seeds, lime segments, coriander and mint, stirring gently to combine. Set aside at room temperature to allow the flavours to infuse.

2 Place the flour in a separate bowl and stir in the cayenne and salt. Use to coat the squid, shaking off any excess. Deep-fry for a minute or two until crisp and golden – you may have to do this in batches. Remove with a slotted spoon and drain on kitchen paper. Arrange mounds of the mango salad in the middle of serving plates and pile the deep-fried squid on top. Serve immediately.

5 Greek Salad with Baked Feta Cheese

JAMES MARTIN'S STARTER

Serves 2

150 g/5 oz feta cheese, halved

2 garlic cloves, finely chopped

2 tsp fresh thyme leaves

5 tbsp extra virgin olive oil

juice of ½ lemon

1 tbsp chopped fresh flat-leaf parsley

2 ripe tomatoes, seeded and chopped

1 small red onion, chopped

115 g/4 oz pitted black olives (good quality)

1 mini cucumber, roughly chopped

salt and freshly ground black pepper

I've given this refreshing and healthy Greek salad a twist with the baked feta topping. This is absolutely delicious served on its own with plenty of crusty bread to mop up all the fantastic juices. Just be careful when seasoning as the feta is already quite salty. Alternatively, try the salad piled on to some charred bread, or serve as part of an antipasto platter.

1 Preheat the oven to 220°C/425°F/Gas 7 (fan oven 200°C from cold). Place the two pieces of feta side by side in a shallow ovenproof dish. Sprinkle over the garlic and thyme, then season with black pepper. Drizzle over two tablespoons of the oil and bake for 6–8 minutes until heated through and slightly bubbling.

2 To make the dressing, place the remaining oil in a bowl and whisk in the lemon juice and parsley. Season to taste. Place the tomatoes, onion, olives and cucumber in the bowl and gently turn in the dressing. Arrange on serving plates and spoon over the baked feta cheese. Serve at once.

6 Marinated Shiitake Parcels

PHIL VICKERY'S STARTER

Serves 2

225 g/8 oz shiitake mushrooms, stalks trimmed

juice of 1 lime

2 tsp white wine

2 tsp balsamic vinegar

1 tbsp olive oil

dash of sesame oil

1 tbsp chopped fresh coriander

salt and freshly ground black pepper

Shiitake mushrooms have a distinctive, almost meaty scent and flavour. Washing will make them waterlogged, so use as they are or give them a quick wipe with a piece of damp kitchen paper. They are excellent with oriental flavours, which makes this a great starter with all its fresh clean tastes. These parcels could also be served as a side order for a larger meal.

1 Preheat the oven to 220°C/425°F/Gas 7 (fan oven 200°C from cold). Cut two 20 cm/8 in squares of foil and divide the shiitake mushrooms between them. Scrunch up the sides so you have containers and sprinkle over the lime juice, white wine and balsamic vinegar. Season generously, then drizzle over the olive oil and add a few drops of sesame oil to each parcel. Finally scatter over the coriander and scrunch up the sides of the foil squares to form parcels.

2 Place the foil parcels on a baking sheet and bake for 8 minutes until the mushrooms are tender. Remove the parcels from the oven and transfer to warmed serving plates. Serve immediately, allowing guests to open their own parcels at the table.

7 Broccoli Tempura with Ginger Dipping Sauce

BRIAN TURNER'S STARTER

Serves 2

sunflower oil, for deep-frying

5 tbsp dark soy sauce

1 tbsp dry sherry or sake (optional)

2 tsp freshly grated root ginger

115 g/4 oz plain flour, plus extra for dusting

1 egg yolk

about 120 ml/4 fl oz ice-cold water

225 g/8 oz broccoli florets (long-stemmed if possible)

salt and freshly ground black pepper

I made this for *Holby City* actress Lisa Faulkner who just loved Japanese food. Perfect tempura should have a thin, almost transparent coating of lightly browned, crisp batter, perfectly balanced in flavour with the vegetable inside. Long thin florets of broccoli work best as anything too broad is in danger of holding water from the batter, resulting in a raw or half-cooked flavour.

1 Preheat a deep-fat fryer or a deep-sided pan one-third full of sunflower oil to 190°C/375°F. To make the dipping sauce, mix together the soy sauce, dry sherry or sake, if using, and ginger in a bowl and dilute with a little cold water to taste. Pour into individual dipping bowls and set to one side.

2 Tip the flour into a bowl and make a well in the centre. Add the egg yolk and gradually whisk in the ice-cold water until the batter reaches the consistency of single cream, then season it.

3 Drop pieces of the broccoli into the batter, lift them out with tongs or your fingers, shaking off any excess, then quickly lower them gently into the hot oil – you'll have to do this in batches.

4 Cook the tempura for 2 minutes, separating and turning the pieces when necessary, until the coating is crisp. Remove with a slotted spoon on to a plate lined with kitchen paper. Arrange on warmed serving plates, square ones if you have them, and serve at once with the bowls of ginger dipping sauce on the side.

8 Tapenade Toasts with Orange and Watercress Salad

LESLEY WATERS'S STARTER

Serves 4

400 g/14 oz can pitted black olives in brine, drained (about 175 g/6 oz in total)

1 tbsp sun-dried tomato paste

1 red chilli, seeded and finely chopped

1 small garlic clove, crushed

about 120 ml/4 fl oz extra virgin olive oil

$\frac{1}{2}$ lemon, pips removed

1 ciabatta or farmhouse-style loaf

2 oranges

85 g/3 oz bag watercress

1 small red onion, halved and very thinly sliced

salt and freshly ground black pepper

These toasts not only look good but are packed full of flavour too. They are a great veggie option for a starter or would make a welcome change as part of a celebration buffet. The olive paste can be prepared in advance, leaving little last-minute preparation.

1 Place the pitted olives in a food processor with the sun-dried tomato paste, chilli, garlic and about four tablespoons of the olive oil. Whizz until blended, then remove the lid and season to taste with a squeeze of lemon juice and black pepper. Transfer to a small bowl with a spatula and set aside until ready to use (or cover with clingfilm and store in the fridge for up to 2 days).

2 Heat a large, heavy-based griddle pan until searing hot. Cut the ciabatta or farmhouse loaf into thick slices, discarding the ends. Add to the pan and toast on both sides, turning them with tongs – you will have to do this in batches. Remove from the pan and drizzle each one with a little of the remaining olive oil.

3 Peel the oranges and then cut into segments, discarding the pith, using a sharp serrated knife. Place in a bowl and add the watercress and red onion, tossing to combine. Season to taste, then add a good squeeze of lemon and a dash of olive oil. Toss until lightly coated. Thickly spread the toasts with the olive paste. Arrange the watercress salad on individual serving plates or one large platter and pile the toasts on top to serve.

9 Artichoke and Bacon Focaccia Toasts

ANTONY WORRALL
THOMPSON'S STARTER

Serves 4–6

290 g jar artichoke hearts in extra virgin olive oil

8 bacon rashers (dry cure, if possible)

4 tbsp roughly chopped fresh flat-leaf parsley

15 g/¹⁄₂ oz fresh basil leaves

115 g/4 oz freshly grated Parmesan shavings

1 focaccia bread, split in half

salt and freshly ground black pepper

These are great served as a starter or handed around with drinks at a barbecue. I must admit I'm not a real fan of canned artichokes or hearts; they are pretty tasteless. However, wood-roasted artichoke hearts in olive oil are very pleasant and make an excellent antipasto piled on to toast. The artichoke mixture would also work well stirred into cooked pasta with a little oil.

1 Heat a frying pan. Drain the oil from the artichoke hearts and reserve, then cut the hearts into slices and place in a bowl. Set aside.

2 Add a little of the reserved artichoke oil to the heated frying pan and fry the bacon until just crisp. Drain on kitchen paper, then when cool enough to handle cut into strips, discarding the rind and any excess fat.

3 Add the bacon strips to the artichoke slices and then add the parsley, basil and Parmesan shavings with a little of the reserved artichoke oil to bind. Mix gently to combine and season to taste.

4 Preheat a griddle pan over a medium-high heat until it is smoking hot, then drizzle with a little of the reserved artichoke oil. Place one half of the focaccia on the grill and toast until nicely marked on the cut side. Keep warm and repeat with the other half of the focaccia.

5 Cut the warm focaccia halves into wedges and carefully pile some of the artichoke and bacon mixture on to each one. Arrange on serving plates or on one large platter and serve at once.

10 Cashel Blue Cheese Soufflés

ROSS BURDEN'S STARTER

Serves 2

25 g/1 oz unsalted butter, plus extra for greasing

25 g/1 oz plain flour

120 ml/4 fl oz milk

2 eggs (preferably organic or free-range)

50 g/2 oz Cashel blue cheese

salt and freshly ground black pepper

These rich little soufflés are much simpler to make than they appear. I made them for Victoria Smurfit, who came on the celebrity version of the show. She had brought along the Cashel blue cheese to reflect her Irish roots and a very good choice it was too: a semi-soft farmhouse blue cheese made from unpasteurized cows' milk in County Tipperary. It is now widely available in the UK in supermarkets and specialist stores. However, the soufflés would be good with any soft blue cheese, such as Gorgonzola or dolcelatte.

1 Preheat the oven to 220°C/425°F/Gas 7 (fan oven 200°C from cold). Lightly butter the insides of two 120 ml/4 fl oz ramekins. Melt the butter in a small pan, stir in the flour and cook over a low heat for 1 minute. Remove from the heat and gradually add the milk, little by little, stirring well after each addition. Return to the heat and cook for 4–5 minutes until smooth and shiny, stirring occasionally.

2 Allow the white sauce to cool slightly, then separate the eggs; place the egg whites in a bowl and set aside. Crumble the Cashel blue cheese into the white sauce and stir in the egg yolks to combine. Season to taste. Using an electric beater, whisk the egg whites until stiff peaks form. Beat a third of the egg whites into the Cashel blue mixture until just blended, then add the rest and gently fold in.

3 Divide the mixture between the prepared ramekins and place them on a baking sheet. Bake for 8–10 minutes until cooked through, well risen and golden brown – avoid opening the oven door during cooking time. Transfer the soufflés on to serving plates and serve immediately – they don't hang around!

11 Deep-fried Brie with Red Onion and Tomato Jam

KEVIN WOODFORD'S
STARTER

Serves 2

sunflower oil, for deep-frying

175 g/6 oz brie wedge

85 g/3 oz seasoned flour

2 eggs (preferably organic or free-range)

115 g/4 oz fresh white breadcrumbs

lightly dressed mixed salad leaves, to serve

FOR THE JAM:

1 tsp sunflower oil

1 small red onion, finely chopped

1 garlic clove, finely chopped

2 ripe tomatoes, peeled, seeded and finely chopped

25 g/1 oz light muscovado sugar

2 tbsp clear honey

1 tbsp white wine vinegar

salt and freshly ground black pepper

This is a great little starter or snack that goes beautifully with a well-dressed selection of leaves. I love the combination of soft, runny brie in a crisp coating and the sweet home-made jam. Even more so than many other recipes, it is the quality of the ingredients that counts. Make sure your brie is ripe but not too runny and that the tomatoes were grown for flavour.

1 Preheat a deep-fat fryer or a deep-sided pan one-third full of sunflower oil to 190°C/375°F. To make the jam, heat the oil in a small pan. Add the onion and sauté for 1–2 minutes to soften. Stir in the garlic and cook for 30 seconds or so, then tip in the tomatoes and cook for another 2 minutes, stirring occasionally.

2 Stir the sugar into the pan with the honey and vinegar, then cook for 1–2 minutes or until the sugar has completely dissolved. Season to taste and simmer gently for 5–10 minutes until well reduced and slightly sticky, stirring occasionally. Remove from the heat and allow to cool.

3 Cut the wedge of brie into 6 even-sized triangles and toss in the seasoned flour. Beat the eggs in a shallow dish and add the dusted brie triangles, turning to coat, then coat them in the breadcrumbs. Arrange on a baking sheet and chill for 5 minutes to firm up (up to 24 hours is fine, if time allows).

4 When you are ready to serve, deep-fry the coated brie triangles for 2–3 minutes until crisp and golden brown. Remove with a slotted spoon and drain on kitchen paper. Arrange the deep-fried brie on serving plates with the salad and serve the jam on the side.

12 Broccoli and Cheddar Soup

AINSLEY HARRIOTT'S SOUP

Serves 4–6

40 g/1½ oz unsalted butter

1 large onion, finely chopped

225 g/8 oz potato, finely diced

900 ml/1½ pints vegetable stock

675 g/1½ lb broccoli head, trimmed and finely chopped

150 g/5 oz mature Cheddar, finely grated

salt and freshly ground black pepper

about 4 tbsp double cream, to serve

I got the inspiration for this recipe on my travels in America, where there is quite a tradition of putting cheese in soup. I love soup – it reminds me of my mum, who used to make it for us on a cold winter's evening. As soon as we got in from school we'd get a big steaming bowl set in front of us with Mum saying, 'That should keep you going until dinner!'

1 Melt the butter in a large pan, add the onion and cook for a few minutes until softened. Stir in the potato and season generously, then cover and cook gently for 10 minutes, shaking the pan occasionally, until the potatoes are just tender.

2 Pour the stock into the pan and bring to the boil, then reduce the heat, add the broccoli and simmer for another 5 minutes or so until the broccoli is just tender. Season to taste.

3 Purée the soup in batches in a food processor and return to the pan, or use a hand-held blender. Stir in the Cheddar and reheat gently for a minute or two until just warmed through. Season to taste and ladle into bowls. Add a swirl of cream to each one and serve at once.

13 Sweet Potato Soup with Sesame Spinach Salad

LESLEY WATERS'S SOUP

Serves 4

25 g/1 oz unsalted butter

1 onion, chopped

2 tsp ground coriander

675 g/1½ lb sweet potatoes, finely chopped

1.2 litres/2 pints vegetable stock

FOR THE SALAD:

2 handfuls baby spinach leaves, roughly shredded

1 tbsp sesame seeds, toasted

1 tsp sesame oil

1½ tsp dark soy sauce

1 red chilli, seeded and very finely chopped

salt and freshly ground black pepper

There are now a number of different varieties of sweet potatoes available, with skins ranging in colour from orange and pink to purple, and the flesh either creamy white or orange. Fortunately they all taste pretty similar, but I normally go for the orange-fleshed variety for that more dramatic colour. I have garnished this soup with a sesame spinach salad, which looks stunning and really needs nothing more than some spinach and a cleverly stocked store cupboard.

1 Heat the butter in a large pan. Add the onion and cook for 5 minutes until softened but not coloured. Stir in the ground coriander with the sweet potatoes and cook for 1 minute.

2 Pour the stock into the pan and season with black pepper. Bring to the boil and simmer for about 15 minutes or until the sweet potatoes are cooked through and tender.

3 Meanwhile, place the baby spinach in a bowl and add the sesame seeds, sesame oil, soy and chilli, tossing to combine. Season to taste and set aside.

4 Transfer the soup to a food processor in batches and whizz until smooth, then pour back into the pan; or use a hand-held blender. Reheat gently, then season to taste. Ladle into four warmed bowls and top each with a generous handful of dressed spinach salad. Eat immediately.

14 Red Onion Soup with Goats' Cheese Croutes

NICK NAIRN'S SOUP

Serves 2

1 tbsp olive oil

knob of unsalted butter

2 red onions, finely diced

1 tsp plain flour

2 tbsp red wine

2 tsp tomato purée

**500 ml/18 fl oz beef stock
salt and freshly ground black
pepper**

FOR THE CROUTES:

**2 thick slices French stick, cut
on the diagonal**

1 tbsp olive oil

50 g/2 oz goats' cheese log

I love soup and often make it on the show; it's almost become a bit of a running joke. The great thing is there is always something in the fridge to rustle up. This recipe worked particularly well with toasted bubbling croutes, the freshness of the cheese cutting through the richness of the soup perfectly. If you haven't got any goats' cheese, use any Swiss cheese or try an equal mixture of Gruyère and Parmesan.

1 Heat the oil in a pan and add the butter. Once it stops sizzling, tip in the onions and cook for 8–10 minutes until softened and lightly browned, stirring occasionally. Season with plenty of black pepper.

2 Stir the flour into the onions and cook for 1 minute, then pour in the wine and cook for another minute, stirring. Mix the tomato purée with the stock and then pour into the pan, stirring to combine. Bring to the boil, then reduce the heat to a simmer for 8–10 minutes or until thickened and slightly reduced.

3 Meanwhile, make the goats' cheese croutes. Preheat the grill and a griddle pan. Drizzle the bread with the oil and griddle for 2 minutes on each side or until lightly charred. Cut the goats' cheese into two even-sized slices and place one on top of each piece of bread.

4 Season the soup to taste and ladle into flameproof soup tureens. Float a goats' cheese croute on each one and place under the grill for a minute or two until the cheese is bubbling and melted. Serve at once.

15 Sweetcorn Soup with Tomato Salsa

PAUL RANKIN'S SOUP

Serves 2–4

500 ml/18 fl oz chicken stock

350 g/12 oz sweetcorn kernels

100 ml/3½ fl oz double cream

FOR THE SALSA:

1 ripe plum tomato, peeled, seeded and finely diced

4 spring onions, finely chopped

1 green chilli, seeded and finely chopped

2 tbsp chopped fresh coriander

salt and freshly ground black pepper

This soup is wonderfully sweet, rich and full of flavour. The addition of the tomato salsa helps spice up the mild delicacy of the sweetcorn, creating the perfect balance. Fresh, frozen or canned sweetcorn kernels all work well, so use whatever's available. In summer, when sweetcorn is at its best, this also makes a delicious chilled soup.

1 Place the stock in a small pan with the sweetcorn and bring to a simmer, then reduce the heat and simmer gently for 4–5 minutes until tender. Transfer to a food processor and blend to a purée, or use a hand-held blender. The mixture will not be completely smooth, but this improves the texture. Return the soup to the pan and stir in the cream. Season to taste, and heat through.

2 Meanwhile, prepare the salsa. Place the tomato in a bowl with the spring onions, chilli and coriander. Stir to combine and season to taste. Ladle the soup into warmed serving bowls and place a spoonful of salsa on top. Serve immediately.

16 Pea and Mint Soup

KEVIN WOODFORD'S SOUP

Serves 4

50 g/2 oz unsalted butter

1 onion, finely chopped

2 garlic cloves, crushed

1 green chilli, seeded and finely chopped

450 g/1 lb bag frozen peas

pinch of sugar

900 ml/1½ pints vegetable or chicken stock

2 tbsp chopped fresh mint, plus extra leaves to garnish

salt and freshly ground black pepper

softly whipped cream, to serve

This is the sort of soup that pleads to be eaten when you are feeling tired and jaded. It is as instant as you are ever going to get and is brilliant if you've got almost nothing in the house. After all, everyone has a bag of frozen peas lurking in the freezer. I love the vibrant green colour and silky texture, and the chilli gives it a surprising and pleasant kick.

1 Melt the butter in a large pan and add the onion, garlic and chilli. Sauté for 3–4 minutes until softened but not coloured. Add the peas and sugar, then pour in the stock and season generously. Bring to the boil, then reduce the heat and simmer for about 5 minutes or until the peas are completely tender.

2 Add the mint to the soup and blend to a purée in a food processor or with a hand-held blender. Reheat gently in the pan and season to taste. Ladle into bowls and add swirls of cream and mint leaves to garnish. Serve immediately.

17 Watercress Soup

JAMES MARTIN'S SOUP

Serves 2

50 g/2 oz unsalted butter

1 red onion, thinly sliced

2 large garlic cloves, finely chopped

600 ml/1 pint vegetable stock

120 ml/4 fl oz double cream

120 ml/4 fl oz milk

400 g/14 oz bunch of water- cress or 2 x 125 g/4½ oz bags

salt and freshly ground black pepper

fresh mint sprigs, to garnish

This soup is great served warm, but it is also excellent chilled and garnished with olive-oil-and-mint ice cubes – literally, olive oil frozen with tiny mint sprigs in ice-cube trays! I love watercress. I live near the famous watercress farms in Hampshire where it is grown in pure spring water; not only does it taste great with its peppery edge, it is also very good for you. Don't be tempted to overcook the watercress or it will lose its wonderful, vibrant green colour.

1 Melt the butter in a pan and add the onion. Cook for 2 minutes until just beginning to soften but not colour, stirring occasionally. Add the garlic and cook for another 2 minutes, stirring.

2 Pour the stock into the pan with the cream and milk. Season to taste and cook for a further 2 minutes until the liquid is just beginning to simmer. Trim the bunch of watercress and remove any thick stalks and discoloured leaves, then chop up and add to the pan. Simmer for 1 minute – any longer and the watercress will start to lose its colour.

3 Purée the soup in batches in a food processor and return to the pan, or use a hand-held blender. Season to taste and reheat gently to warm through, then ladle into warmed serving bowls and garnish with mint sprigs to serve.

18 Wild Mushroom and Stilton Soup

PHIL VICKERY'S SOUP

Serves 2

1 stale slice country-style bread

600 ml/1 pint vegetable or chicken stock

1 garlic clove, crushed

4 spring onions, thinly sliced

150 g/5 oz mixed wild mushrooms, wiped clean and finely chopped (such as chanterelle, shiitake and blewit)

50 ml/2 fl oz double cream or milk

85 g/3 oz Stilton, diced

1 tbsp each roughly chopped fresh chervil, flat-leaf parsley and tarragon

salt and freshly ground black pepper

Soup made from wild mushrooms has the most extraordinarily intense flavour. It also works well with wild mushrooms that are a few days old and have darkened a bit. If you are watching what you eat, omit the cream and use milk instead. Just be careful not to overcook the Stilton or it will become stringy and rubbery.

1 Moisten the bread with a little water and leave to soak for a few minutes. Place the stock in a pan with the garlic and spring onions and bring to a simmer. Squeeze out the excess moisture from the bread, tear into pieces and add to the simmering stock with the mushrooms. Season with pepper, reduce the heat and simmer gently for 5–6 minutes or until the mushrooms are tender.

2 Ladle the soup into a food processor, blend to a purée and return to the pan; or use a hand-held blender. Season to taste and reheat gently. Stir in the cream or milk, and whisk in the Stilton. Cook for another minute until the Stilton is completely melted, stirring, then add the herbs. Ladle the soup into warmed bowls to serve.

19 Thai Fragrant Chicken Soup

Serves 2

1 tbsp olive oil

1 shallot, finely chopped

1 red chilli, finely chopped

40 g/1½ oz chestnut mush-
rooms, thinly sliced

50 g/2 oz chicken fillet,
shredded

450 ml/¾ pint chicken stock

1 lemongrass stalk, trimmed
and bruised

2 kaffir lime leaves

25 g/1 oz fresh Thai basil

juice of 1 lime

This spicy soup will revive your senses at the end of the day. It appears in some form on every Thai restaurant menu in the country, but I like the fresh flavours of this version. Once you've mastered the basic method you can experiment with your own choice of ingredients. For a special occasion try a mixture of scallops, mussels and squid. Thai basil is available in Asian supermarkets and often has a slight red tinge. You could always substitute with a mixture of ordinary basil and coriander.

1 Heat the olive oil in a pan. Add the shallot and sauté for 2 minutes until softened but not coloured. Stir in the chilli and mushrooms and sauté for another 2 minutes.

2 Tip the shredded chicken fillet into the pan and continue to cook for 2–3 minutes or until the chicken is sealed and just tender. Pour in the chicken stock and add the lemongrass and kaffir lime leaves. Bring to the boil, then simmer for 8 minutes or until the flavours are well combined and the soup has slightly reduced.

3 Just before serving, quickly shred the Thai basil leaves, discarding the stalks, and stir into the soup with the lime juice. Remove from the heat and ladle into Thai-style bowls. Serve immediately.

20 Prawn and Chorizo Broth

TONY TOBIN'S SOUP

Serves 2

6 raw whole king prawns (heads and shells intact)

1 tbsp olive oil

600 ml/1 pint chicken or fish stock

1 small red onion, finely diced

1 small chorizo, skinned and finely diced (about 50 g/2 oz in total)

1 large potato, finely diced

pinch of dried chilli flakes

pinch of ground turmeric

2 plum tomatoes, peeled, seeded and diced

2 tbsp chopped mixed fresh herbs (such as flat-leaf parsley and coriander)

salt and freshly ground black pepper

country-style crusty bread, to serve (optional)

I don't often make soups on *Ready Steady Cook* as I don't think they are very visual, so this one was an exception. Its origins are definitely Spanish so I called it 'Paella broth' on the show. Try to skim off the oil that gathers on top of the soup as it is cooking. I find one of the easiest ways of doing this is to gently lay a piece of absorbent kitchen paper on top, where it will soak up the oil.

1 Heat a lidded pan. To prepare the prawns, break off the heads, then take off the shells and remove the veins. Set the prawns aside. Add a little of the oil to the heated pan and tip in the prawn heads and shells. Cook for 1 minute, stirring, then pour in the stock and bring to a simmer. Reduce the heat and simmer for 10 minutes to allow the flavours to infuse.

2 Meanwhile, heat the remaining oil in a separate pan. Add the onion and cook, stirring, for 2–3 minutes until softened but not coloured. Tip in the chorizo and cook for another 2–3 minutes or until the chorizo is sizzling and has begun to release its natural oils. Stir in the potatoes and continue to cook for another minute until well coated, then stir in the chilli flakes and turmeric and cook for 1 minute, stirring. Season generously.

3 Strain the prawn-infused stock through a fine sieve into the onion and chorizo mixture, stirring to combine. Return to a simmer, stir in the tomatoes, then reduce the heat and cook for another 5 minutes or so, until the potato is completely tender but still holding its shape, skimming off any excess fat.

4 Remove the pan from the heat, stir in the raw peeled prawns, cover and set aside for 3–4 minutes to allow the prawns to cook and turn opaque. Stir in the herbs and season to taste, then ladle into warmed serving bowls and serve with some crusty bread on the side, if liked.

21 Mussel and Saffron Soup

ANTONY WORRALL
THOMPSON'S SOUP

Serves 4–6

50 g/2 oz unsalted butter

1 leek, trimmed and finely chopped

2 garlic cloves, finely chopped

2 tsp finely chopped fresh root ginger

500 ml/18 fl oz dry white wine

2 kg/4½ lb mussels, cleaned

500 ml/18 fl oz fish stock

1 small potato, diced

1 small carrot, diced

1 celery stick, diced

1 bay leaf

1 fresh thyme sprig

pinch of saffron stamens, soaked in 1 tbsp warm water

300 ml/½ pint double cream

salt and freshly ground black pepper

When I made this on the programme I called it 'Ménage à Trois' after my first London restaurant where it was always on the menu. It has to be one of the nicest combinations I know, with the saffron stamens providing a wonderful pale yellow colour to the soup. Serve it with some warm crusty French bread slathered with butter – delicious!

1 Heat the butter in a large pan with a tight-fitting lid. Add the leek, garlic and ginger and cook over a low heat until softened but not browned. Transfer half of the leek mixture to a second pan and set aside. Add the wine to the first pan and bring to the boil. Tip in the mussels, cover and cook over a high heat for a few minutes, shaking the pan occasionally, until all the mussels have opened (discard any that do not open).

2 Strain the mussels through a colander set over a large bowl. Remove the meat from the mussels and reserve. Strain the reserved cooking liquor through a fine sieve into the second pan, leaving behind any grit. Add the fish stock, potato, carrot, celery, bay leaf and thyme, bring to the boil and simmer for 10 minutes.

3 Remove the bay leaf and thyme from the soup and purée in batches in a food processor, then return to the pan; or use a hand-held blender. Stir in the saffron stamens with the cream. Season to taste and reheat gently but do not allow to boil. Add the mussels and warm through, stirring. Ladle the soup into warmed serving bowls and serve at once.

22 Kipper Chowder

ROSS BURDEN'S SOUP

Serves 4

600 ml/1 pint milk

1 kipper fillet (undyed, if possible)

1 bay leaf

40 g/1½ oz unsalted butter

25 g/1 oz plain flour

2 tbsp white wine

225 g/8 oz fresh spinach, cleaned

115 g/4 oz cooked mashed potato

50 g/2 oz Cheddar, grated

1 garlic clove, finely chopped

about 50 ml/2 fl oz double cream

salt and freshly ground black pepper

A bowl of soup must be one of the most welcoming foods known to man. This comforting chowder always goes down well when it is bitterly cold outside. It uses kipper as the main ingredient, which was once of the best loved fish in the whole of the British Isles but now, sadly, seems to have fallen out of favour. I really like kipper's distinctive flavour, but this recipe happened almost by accident on the show – and was a revelation.

1 Place the milk in a sauté pan and add the kipper and bay leaf. Cook gently for 3–4 minutes until just tender, then allow to cool slightly. Discard the bay leaf and transfer the kipper to a plate, then flake, discarding any skin and bone.

2 Strain the poaching milk into a jug. Melt 25 g/1 oz of the butter in a pan, stir in the flour and cook over a low heat for 1 minute. Remove from the heat and gradually add the poaching milk, little by little, stirring until smooth after each addition. Return to the heat and cook for 4–5 minutes until thickened and smooth, stirring occasionally.

3 Meanwhile, heat a pan and add the remaining knob of butter. Once it stops sizzling, pour in the wine and allow it to bubble down. Tip in the spinach and cook for 1–2 minutes, keeping it moving around with a spatula or by shaking the pan. Season to taste, then drain off any excess liquid. Tip into a clean tea towel and squeeze out the excess liquid, then roughly chop.

4 Mix the mashed potato into the cooked white sauce until well combined, then stir in the Cheddar and garlic. Cook for a minute or so until the cheese is melted, stirring. Stir in the spinach with the kipper flakes and cream, then cook gently until just warmed through. Season to taste and ladle into warmed serving bowls. Serve immediately.

23 Aubergine Caviar Bruschetta

NICK NAIRN'S
SNACK/LIGHT BITE

Serves 2

5 tbsp olive oil

1 aubergine, peeled and finely diced

1 small red onion, finely chopped

6 thick slices ciabatta bread, cut on the diagonal

2 tbsp chopped fresh coriander

1 tbsp snipped fresh chives

sea salt and freshly ground black pepper

lime wedges, to garnish

This aubergine 'caviar' is ideal warm or cold as a dip, or hot as a garnish for lamb or salmon. It is a variation on *baba ganoush*, which I'm told means 'spoilt old man' in Arabic. I have served it here with chargrilled ciabatta but any rustic bread would work well. It makes a delicious snack, or serve it as a light lunch or vegetarian starter with some lightly dressed tomato and baby leaf salad on the side. It will keep for up to three days in a sealed container in the fridge.

1 Heat three tablespoons of the olive oil in a frying pan and then tip in the aubergine. Cook for about 5 minutes until just beginning to soften and colour. Season generously, add the onion, then continue to sauté for 4–5 minutes or until the onion is softened and tender, stirring occasionally.

2 Meanwhile, heat a griddle pan until it is smoking hot. Drizzle the remaining oil over the slices of bread, sprinkle with sea salt and toast on the griddle pan until nicely marked on both sides.

3 Stir the coriander and chives into the aubergine mixture and transfer to a serving bowl set on a plate. Garnish with the lime wedges and serve warm or cold with the hot chargrilled bread.

24 Potato and Bacon Rösti with Poached Egg

AINSLEY HARRIOTT'S
SNACK/LIGHT BITE

Serves 4

2 x 200 g/7 oz waxy potatoes, unpeeled (such as Maris Piper)

25 g/1 oz unsalted butter

1 small onion, finely chopped

2 rindless streaky bacon rashers, finely chopped

about 1 tbsp white wine vinegar

4 large eggs (preferably organic or free-range)

sunflower oil, for shallow-frying

2 tbsp chopped fresh flat-leaf parsley

about 25 g/1 oz plain flour, sifted

salt and freshly cracked black pepper

fresh whole chives, to garnish

Crisp on the outside, soft and buttery inside, these röstis will help you get over the worst of hangovers. I also like to serve them as a light supper dish. They can happily be made up to four hours in advance and left at room temperature until you are ready to eat, then, rather than shallow-frying, bake them in a preheated oven at 180°C/350°F/Gas 4 (fan oven 160°C from cold) for 8–10 minutes until heated through.

1 Steam the potatoes over a pan of boiling water for 10 minutes, then remove from the heat and leave until cool enough to handle. Melt the butter in a frying pan and cook the onion for a couple of minutes until softened. Add the bacon and continue to cook until the bacon is just crisp. Remove from the heat.

2 Heat a large pan with plenty of salted water. Add the vinegar and bring to the boil. Break each egg into the water where it is bubbling, then turn the heat down and simmer gently for 1 minute. Remove each egg with a slotted spoon and plunge into a bowl of iced water. When cold trim down any ragged ends from the cooked egg white; return to the bowl of iced water until ready to use.

3 Heat enough oil to shallow-fry in a large frying pan. Peel the cooked potatoes and coarsely grate into a bowl. Stir in the onion and bacon mixture and the parsley and season generously, then add just enough flour to bind. Divide into eight equal portions and shape each one into a pancake about 2.5 cm/1 in thick. Shallow-fry the röstis for about 3–4 minutes on each side until golden brown and cooked through. Drain on kitchen paper. Return the poached eggs to a pan of boiling salted water for 30 seconds or until just heated through.

4 Arrange two of the potato and bacon röstis on each warmed serving plate. Lift the poached eggs out of the water and drain briefly on kitchen paper, then place one on each double portion of rösti. Garnish with a sprinkling of cracked black pepper and some criss-crossed whole chives to serve.

25 Roasted Red Pepper, Mozzarella and Spinach Croutes

TONY TOBIN'S
SNACK/LIGHT BITE

Serves 4

50 g/2 oz unsalted butter

about 2 tbsp olive oil

2 soda farls, each cut into 5 slices

2 garlic cloves, finely chopped

115 g/4 oz frozen spinach cubes, defrosted at room temperature

2 canned whole pimientos (sweet red peppers), drained and rinsed

150 g/5 oz ball of mozzarella, drained

salt and freshly ground black pepper

This is a posh title for toasted cheese sandwiches. As my mum is Irish I've developed a fondness for soda farls, which we often have in the house. This recipe is really a great store-cupboard standby; but roasted or sautéed red peppers would also work very well, as would some lightly cooked fresh spinach. It just depends on what you've got to hand. I suppose they're like mini pizzas, and are perfect if you are looking for something tasty in a hurry.

1 Preheat the grill to medium. Heat a frying pan over a medium heat and add the butter and a little of the oil. Once it stops sizzling, add the soda farl slices and cook for a minute or two on each side until lightly golden – you'll have to do this in batches. Transfer to a plate and set aside.

2 Add a tablespoon of the oil to the same pan. Stir in the garlic and cook for 30 seconds, then add the spinach and continue to cook for 1–2 minutes until heated through, stirring. Season to taste. Cut the pimientos into small pieces and chop up the mozzarella to roughly the same size. Place both in a bowl and stir gently to combine.

3 Spoon the spinach mixture on to the toasted croutes and pile the mozzarella and pimiento mixture on top. Season to taste and add a light drizzle of oil to each one. Place on the grill rack and toast for 1–2 minutes or until the cheese is bubbling and lightly golden. Arrange on warmed serving plates and enjoy!

26 Wok Omelette with Green Basil Sauce and Crispy Parma Ham

LESLEY WATERS'S
SNACK/LIGHT BITE

Serves 2

50 g/2 oz bunch of fresh basil, stalks discarded

6 tbsp extra virgin olive oil

4 eggs (preferably organic or free-range)

8 thin slices Parma ham, about 115 g/4 oz in total

1 tsp softened unsalted butter

85 g/3 oz bag of baby salad leaves

½ lemon, pips removed

salt and freshly ground black pepper

This stylish dish mostly uses ingredients from the *Ready Steady Cook* store cupboard, with the exception of the Parma ham, which could always be substituted with bacon, and the salad leaves. The omelette is a complete variation on a traditional recipe and must be made in a non-stick wok.

1 Using a hand-held blender or mini food processor, whizz the basil leaves with four tablespoons of the olive oil. Season to taste and set side.

2 Crack the eggs into a small bowl and whisk until lightly beaten, then season generously.

3 Heat another tablespoon of the oil in a frying pan and add the Parma ham in batches. Fry for 2–3 minutes until crisp and lightly golden, turning once. Drain on kitchen paper.

4 Heat a wok, then add the butter and swirl around the sides until foaming. Pour in the egg mixture and gently swirl around the surface of the wok. Cook for a minute or two until golden brown underneath, but still slightly soft and runny on the top.

5 Divide the salad leaves between two serving plates and dress with the remaining tablespoon of olive oil and a squeeze of lemon juice. Cut the omelette roughly into four pieces using two wooden spatulas, and arrange on the salad. Spoon over the green basil sauce and place the crispy Parma ham on top to serve.

27 Pea and Onion Bhajis

PHIL VICKERY'S
SNACK/LIGHT BITE

Serves 4

sunflower oil, for deep-frying

¼ tsp each cumin seeds, dried chilli flakes and cracked black pepper

115 g/4 oz self-raising flour

1 tsp ground turmeric

½ tsp each ground paprika and salt

1 bunch of spring onions, shredded (about 6 in total)

115 g/4 oz frozen peas, thawed

1 lime, cut into wedges, to garnish

selection of chutneys and pickles, to serve (optional)

Real onion bhajis are made using gram (chickpea) flour but I improvised by using regular self-raising flour and colouring it with turmeric and paprika. These are delicious served on their own with a squeeze of lime; a selection of your favourite chutneys and pickles would also work a treat.

1 Preheat a deep-fat fryer or a deep-sided pan one-third full of sunflower oil to 190°C/375°F. Heat a small frying pan and dry-fry the cumin seeds, chilli flakes and pepper for 30 seconds until aromatic.

2 Place the flour in a bowl with the turmeric, paprika and salt, then tip in the toasted spices. Stir to combine, then mix in about 150 ml/¼ pint of cold water to make a smooth thick batter. Stir in the spring onions and peas until well coated.

3 Carefully drop the mixture into the heated oil using two tablespoons – one to scoop up the batter and the other to push it into the oil; you may have to do this in batches. Deep-fry for 4–5 minutes until crisp and golden brown, turning occasionally with tongs. Drain on kitchen paper, then pile on to a warmed serving platter. Serve immediately with the lime wedges and selection of chutneys and pickles, if liked.

28 Quesadilla Triangles with Refried Beans

ANTONY WORRALL
THOMPSON'S
SNACK/LIGHT BITE

Serves 2–4

2 tbsp olive oil, plus extra for brushing

1 small red onion, finely chopped

1 garlic clove, finely chopped

good pinch of dried chilli flakes

400 g/14 oz can mixed beans, drained and rinsed

juice of 1 lime

4 tbsp chopped fresh coriander, plus extra leaves to garnish

8 soft flour tortillas

225 g/8 oz Cheddar or Cheshire cheese, grated

about 120 ml/4 fl oz soured cream or thick Greek yoghurt

salt and freshly ground black pepper

These quesadilla triangles are addictive and make the perfect snack for the whole family to enjoy. They can be prepared up to one hour in advance, covered with clingfilm and kept at room temperature. You can vary the fillings depending on what's available, but Mexican pepper salsa with Gruyère works well, as does plain cheese garnished with some spicy guacamole.

1 Preheat the oven to 200°C/400°F/Gas 6 (fan oven 180°C from cold). Heat the olive oil in a frying pan. Add the onion, garlic and chilli flakes and cook for 3–4 minutes until softened but not coloured, stirring. Add the beans and continue to sauté for a few minutes until heated through, stirring occasionally. Remove the pan from the heat and add the lime juice, then stir in the coriander and season to taste.

2 Meanwhile, heat a griddle pan over a medium heat until very hot. Brush one side of a tortilla with a little oil. Place the tortilla in the pan, oiled-side down, and cook for 1 minute until nicely marked, pressing down with a spatula. Repeat with the remaining tortillas.

3 Meanwhile, return the pan of beans to the heat and refry for 3–4 minutes until heated through, then roughly mash, leaving some texture in the beans.

4 Arrange half the tortillas on baking sheets, marked-side down, and sprinkle over a tablespoon of the cheese, then spread over some of the refried beans. Sprinkle another tablespoon of the cheese on top and cover with the remaining tortillas, marked-side up. Bake for about 5 minutes or until heated through and the cheese has melted. Allow to cool slightly until easy to handle.

5 Cut each quesadilla into eight wedges with a serrated knife, pizza cutter or kitchen scissors. Garnish each wedge with a small spoonful of soured cream or yoghurt and a coriander leaf. Arrange on warmed serving plates or one large platter to serve.

29 Guinness Pancakes with Crispy Bacon and Cheddar

JAMES MARTIN'S
SNACK/LIGHT BITE

Serves 2

115 g/4 oz plain flour

1 tsp baking powder

$1/2$ tsp fresh thyme leaves

2 eggs (preferably organic or free-range)

about 150 ml/$1/4$ pint Guinness

about 2 tbsp sunflower oil

knob of unsalted butter

6 rindless bacon rashers (dry-cure, if possible)

50 g/2 oz mature Cheddar, grated

2 tbsp chopped mixed fresh herbs (such as chives, flat-leaf parsley and basil)

salt and freshly ground black pepper

In my opinion there's nothing better than the smell of bacon cooking. But don't go skimping on the cost: choose the best dry-cured British bacon money can buy. To make good pancakes, you need to use a good quality heavy-based non-stick frying pan so that the heat is conducted evenly. This would make an excellent brunch dish for a relaxed Sunday (or any other) morning; or try it just in from the pub, and listen to the groans of appreciation from your guests as they tuck in!

1 Preheat the grill and heat a heavy-based frying pan. Sieve the flour into a bowl with the baking powder and a pinch of salt, then stir in the thyme. Break the eggs into a jug with the Guinness, then lightly whisk to combine. Make a well in the centre of the flour and quickly add enough of the Guinness mixture to make a smooth batter – the consistency of thick cream.

2 Add a thin film of oil (one tablespoon) to the heated pan and ladle in spoonfuls of the pancake batter, allowing them to spread out to about 7.5 cm/3 in in diameter. Reduce the heat and cook for 2–3 minutes until small bubbles appear on the surface. Turn over and cook for another 1–2 minutes until the pancakes are lightly golden. Stack on a plate and keep warm. Repeat until you have 8–10 pancakes in total, depending on how hungry you are!

3 Meanwhile, heat a separate large frying pan and add the remaining tablespoon of oil and the knob of butter. Fry the bacon rashers until nice and crisp, turning once. Mix together the cheese and herbs in a small bowl. Arrange the pancakes on a baking sheet, scatter over the cheese mixture and season with pepper. Place under the grill until just beginning to melt, then transfer to warmed serving plates and top with the bacon to serve.

30 Smoked Salmon and Spinach Puff Pizza

PAUL RANKIN'S
SNACK/LIGHT BITE

Serves 4

350 g/12 oz ready-made puff pastry, thawed if frozen

a little plain flour, for dusting

50 g/2 oz unsalted butter

225 g/8 oz fresh spinach, cleaned

pinch of freshly grated nutmeg

1 large egg yolk

115 g/4 oz slices smoked salmon (preferably wild)

4 tbsp double cream

salt and freshly ground black pepper

fresh basil leaves, to garnish

When I devised this on the programme I served it with Eggs Benedict and a creamy herb and shallot sauce. I was so pleased with the results that I put it on the menu at the restaurant. We've now tried it in numerous guises, from diced Mediterranean vegetable to goats' cheese with pesto.

1 Preheat the oven to 220°C/425°F/Gas 7 (fan oven 200°C from cold). Roll out the pastry on a lightly floured board to a 30 cm/12 in circle that is no more than 5 mm/¼ in thick. Place on a baking sheet, then press down on the circle with a pan lid to make an indent, creating a 5 mm/¼ in border. Prick all over with a fork and chill for at least 5 minutes (up to 30 minutes is best).

2 Heat a large heavy-based frying pan over a medium heat. Once the pastry circle has rested, bake it for 8–10 minutes until lightly golden. Add half the butter to the heated pan, and when it has foamed and then subsided, toss in the spinach. Cook for 1–2 minutes, keeping the spinach leaves moving around with a spatula or by shaking the pan, and season with a little salt. Drain off excess liquid, then add the rest of the butter, season and add nutmeg to taste.

3 Remove the pastry disc from the oven and brush with a little of the egg yolk to prevent it from absorbing too much liquid from the spinach, then spread over the spinach and arrange the salmon on top. Mix the rest of the egg yolk in a small bowl with the cream, then brush all over the spinach and salmon mixture. Return the pizza to the oven and bake for about 5–6 minutes or until puffed up and lightly golden. Transfer to a warmed flat serving plate and garnish with the basil leaves. Cut into wedges and serve at once.

31 Stilton Rarebits

BRIAN TURNER'S
SNACK/LIGHT BITE

Serves 2

100 ml/3½ fl oz lager

50 ml/2 fl oz double cream

115 g/4 oz Stilton, crumbled

1 tbsp Dijon mustard

2 egg yolks

8 thick slices farmhouse white bread

sunflower oil, for frying

25 g/1 oz unsalted butter

freshly ground black pepper

lightly dressed baby leaf salad, to serve

Neil Morrissey came on the show to create awareness for his charity War Child – a worthy cause that he puts a great deal of time and effort into. I made this rarebit with some very nice Stilton he brought along. It would be lovely for a light lunch or after-dinner course served with celery sticks and a simple watercress salad. The rarebit mixture will keep covered with clingfilm for up to two days in the fridge.

1 Preheat the oven to 230°C/450°F/Gas 8 (fan oven 210°C from cold). Place the lager in a small pan with the cream and bring to the boil, then reduce the heat and simmer until slightly reduced. Remove from the heat, stir in the Stilton until melted and then stir in the mustard and egg yolks. Season with pepper, then pour into a shallow dish and place in the fridge to chill for at least 5 minutes (up to 2 days in the fridge, covered with clingfilm, is fine), until needed.

2 Using a cooking ring or cutter, stamp out two 6 cm/2½ in circles from each slice of bread. Heat a little oil with the butter in a frying pan and fry the bread circles in batches for a minute or so on each side until lightly golden, then transfer to a baking sheet. Spread over some of the chilled cheese mixture and bake for 2–3 minutes until bubbling and lightly golden. Arrange on warmed serving plates and add a small mound of the salad to serve.

32 Bruschetta with Sardines and Red Pepper Mayonnaise

ROSS BURDEN'S
SNACK/LIGHT BITE

Serves 2

1 red pepper, seeded and quartered

200 ml/7 fl oz olive oil

finely grated rind and juice of 1 small lemon

2 garlic cloves, peeled

1 tbsp chopped fresh flat-leaf parsley

4 fresh sardines, cleaned and filleted

2 egg yolks

120 ml/4 fl oz sunflower oil

2 tsp white wine vinegar

1 tsp caster sugar

1 tsp Dijon mustard

4 slices country-style bread

salt and freshly ground black pepper

lightly dressed wild rocket salad, to serve

Sardines remind me of Euro-railing around Portugal in the summer of 1991. For me, this recipe is next best to sardines grilled over charcoal. Try to use fresh sardines and get your fishmonger to fillet them for you. Here they are served with the Italian version of toast: bruschetta, which is the basis for most snacks in my house.

1 Preheat the grill to medium. Arrange the pepper quarters on the grill rack and cook for 8–10 minutes until the skins are blackened and blistered. Put 50 ml/2 fl oz of the olive oil in a shallow non-metallic dish with the lemon juice. Finely chop one of the garlic cloves and add with the parsley, then season. Tip in the sardines and, using your hands, rub in the marinade. Set aside for at least 5 minutes to marinate (or for up to 30 minutes in the fridge, if time allows).

2 To make the mayonnaise, whisk the egg yolks in a bowl with a pinch of salt. Mix the remaining 150 ml/5 fl oz of olive oil in a jug with the sunflower oil. Add the vinegar to the egg yolks with the sugar, mustard and lemon rind, then very gradually add the mixed oils, a little at a time, stirring constantly until thickened and smooth. Transfer the cooked peppers to a bowl and cover with clingfilm; leave for a few minutes so the steam helps soften the skin, then tear off the skin, place the flesh in a mini food processor and blend it to a purée. Stir into the mayonnaise and season to taste.

3 Heat a large non-stick frying pan. Add the sardines and cook for 1–2 minutes on each side until crusty and golden brown. Arrange the bread slices on the grill rack and grill until toasted, turning once. Cut the remaining garlic clove in half and use to rub one side of each slice of bread. Arrange the sardines on warmed serving plates with the bruschetta and rocket salad. Add a good spoonful of the mayonnaise, serving the rest separately in a serving bowl.

33 Hot-smoked Salmon Kedgeree

KEVIN WOODFORD'S
SNACK/LIGHT BITE

Serves 2

115 g/4 oz long-grain rice

2 eggs (preferably organic or free-range)

50 g/2 oz unsalted butter

1 red onion, finely chopped

1 tsp mild curry paste

225 g/8 oz honey-roast hot-smoked salmon flakes

2 tbsp chopped fresh flat-leaf parsley

50 ml/2 fl oz double cream

salt and freshly ground black pepper

Kedgeree, which has a strong foothold in British culture, originated in India, its name being an anglicized version of the word *kicheri*, a peasant dish of rice and peas. For me, it still conjures up images of days of the Raj, when the Victorians turned it into a fashionable breakfast dish by adding smoked finnan haddock and eggs and leaving out the beans. However, by incorporating hot-smoked salmon, the kedgeree is transformed into a modern brunch dish or a smashing supper fit to grace any table.

1 Place the rice in a pan of boiling salted water and simmer for 10–12 minutes until just tender. Drain, then spread out on a baking sheet and allow to cool completely – this will prevent the rice grains sticking together. Cook the eggs in a small pan of simmering water for 10–12 minutes until hard-boiled. Rinse under cold water and crack away the shells, then chop.

2 Meanwhile, heat the butter in a sauté pan and cook the onion for about 5 minutes until softened but not coloured. Stir in the curry paste and cook for another 30 seconds or so, stirring.

3 Fold the cooled rice into the onion mixture in the pan along with the salmon and cook for a couple of minutes until just warmed through. Stir in the hard-boiled eggs and parsley and season to taste. Lightly whip the cream in a small bowl and gently fold into the rice mixture. Tip the kedgeree into a warmed serving dish and serve immediately.

34 Crispy Onion Rings

AINSLEY HARRIOTT'S
ACCOMPANIMENT

Serves 2–4

1 Spanish onion

300 ml/½ pint milk

sunflower oil, for deep-frying

85 g/3 oz self-raising flour

2 tsp paprika

salt and freshly ground black pepper

For me there's nothing nicer for Sunday lunch than a tender steak, garnished with a huge pile of these crispy onion rings – delicious. They were also a firm favourite of Fern Britton's while she was presenting the show and I was always happy to make them as they are so easy to prepare. The longer you can leave the onions soaking in the milk the better – up to half an hour is fine.

1 Peel the onion and slice into 1 cm/½ in slices, then separate into rings. Place in a bowl and pour over the milk. Set aside at room temperature for at least 5 and up to 30 minutes (the longer the better).

2 Meanwhile, heat 5 cm/2 in of the oil in a wok or sauté pan. Generously season the flour and mix with the paprika, then spread on to a plate. Drain batches of the onion rings and quickly toss in the seasoned flour, shaking off any excess. Deep-fry for 2–3 minutes until crisp and golden brown. Drain on kitchen paper. Pile up into a warmed serving dish and serve immediately.

35 Cumin and Lemon Roasted Carrots

NICK NAIRN'S
ACCOMPANIMENT

Serves 4

1 tbsp olive oil

15 g/½ oz unsalted butter

pinch of cumin seeds

½ tsp dried chilli flakes

350 g/12 oz baby carrots,
scrubbed and trimmed

½ lemon, pips removed

2 tbsp chopped fresh coriander

salt and freshly ground black
pepper

Sometimes it's the simplest things that work best. The aromatic toasted cumin seeds and chilli combine well with the flavour of the carrots to make a delicious vegetable side order for roast new season lamb, best enjoyed in spring – which just happens to be when carrots are at their sweetest. By the way, baby carrots need only be rinsed and brushed gently under a tap to remove any residual soil.

1 Preheat the oven to 220°C/425°F/Gas 7 (fan oven 200°C from cold). Heat the oil and butter in a small ovenproof frying pan, then add the cumin seeds and chilli flakes and cook gently for 1–2 minutes until fragrant.

2 Add the carrots, turning to coat, then season and cook for 2–3 minutes, turning the carrots occasionally. Squeeze the lemon over them, tossing to combine.

3 Transfer the carrots to the oven and cook for another 10–12 minutes or until cooked through and completely tender. Toss in the coriander and pile into a warmed serving dish to serve.

36 Potato and Lentil Risotto with Pecorino

PAUL RANKIN'S
ACCOMPANIMENT

Serves 4

50 g/2 oz unsalted butter

1 red onion, finely chopped

300 g/10 oz potatoes, finely diced

about 600 ml/1 pint vegetable or chicken stock

400 g/14 oz can Puy lentils, drained and rinsed (200 g/7 oz net weight)

dash of balsamic vinegar (optional)

2 tbsp chopped fresh flat-leaf parsley

50 g/2 oz pecorino cheese, finely grated

salt and freshly ground black pepper

This is not a risotto in the true sense of the word but it's made in a similar fashion, hence the name. I made it for Jilly Goolden when she came on the show and it went down particularly well. I still make a version of it occasionally at home and serve it with crispy fried cod, but it would be equally nice with roast duck or pork. Pecorino cheese is made from ewe's milk and has a strong, quite pronounced flavour. Look out for the aged, hard pecorino romano or pecorino sardo, which are perfect to use in this dish.

1 Melt the butter in a large sauté pan and add the onion and potatoes. Cook for 2 minutes, stirring until the onion has softened but not coloured. Pour in enough of the stock to just cover, then bring to the boil. Reduce the heat and simmer gently for 8–10 minutes or until the potatoes are tender and cooked through.

2 Stir the lentils into the pan and cook for another minute or two, stirring, then season to taste and add a dash of balsamic vinegar, if liked. Stir in the parsley, then spoon the risotto into a warmed serving dish and scatter the pecorino over. Serve immediately.

37 Oriental Noodles

ANTONY WORRALL
THOMPSON'S
ACCOMPANIMENT

Serves 4

1 bunch of spring onions, trimmed (about 6 in total)

4 cm/1½ in piece of fresh root ginger

1 vegetable stock cube

225 g/8 oz Chinese egg noodles

2 tbsp sunflower oil

1–2 red chillies, seeded and finely chopped

2 large garlic cloves, finely chopped

2 tbsp dark soy sauce

2 tbsp fresh lime juice

2 tbsp chopped fresh coriander, to serve

This recipe is a wonderful way to spice up otherwise fairly bland noodles, and you can even make this into a noodle broth by simply adding stock. Be careful not to overcook noodles or they become flabby and lose their bite. Use as little or as much chilli as you dare, but take care what you touch after handling them! You could wear rubber or plastic gloves but I have to admit I never bother. I rub my hands with a little oil before preparing the chillies instead.

1 Finely chop the white parts of the spring onions and set aside. Peel and cut three thin slices from the ginger, then finely chop the remainder and set it aside. Add the green onion tops and ginger slices to a pan of water. Crumble in the stock cube and bring to the boil. Add the noodles to the pan and cook for 3 minutes until just tender. Drain thoroughly, removing the spring onions and ginger.

2 Heat a wok or large frying pan over a high heat until searing hot. Add the oil and swirl it around the sides, then tip in the reserved chopped spring onions and ginger with the chilli and garlic. Stir-fry for 1 minute, then fold in the noodles and sprinkle over the soy sauce and lime juice. Continue to stir-fry for another minute or two until heated through. Pile into a warmed serving dish and scatter with the coriander to serve.

38 Chorizo and Artichoke Pilaff

JAMES MARTIN'S
ACCOMPANIMENT

Serves 4

1 tbsp olive oil

knob of unsalted butter

1 small onion, finely chopped

115 g/4 oz chorizo sausage,
thinly sliced

225 g/8 oz long-grain rice

100 ml/3½ fl oz dry white wine

400 ml/14 fl oz chicken stock

115 g/4 oz artichoke hearts
preserved in olive oil, drained
and roughly chopped

4 tbsp chopped fresh flat-leaf
parsley

salt and freshly ground black
pepper

Not surprisingly there are always fashions in food, and recently on the show chorizo seemed to be the Gucci of the moment. For those of you who don't know (and I'm sure there aren't many), chorizo is a spicy Spanish paprika sausage. For cooking, raw is best and it just needs to be sautéed to bring out the wonderful smoky flavours. I served this pilaff with tea-smoked chicken breasts but it would be equally good with a grilled cod fillet or some pan-fried monkfish.

1 Heat the oil and butter in a heavy-based pan with a tight-fitting lid. Add the onion and sauté for about 2 minutes until softened, stirring occasionally. Add the chorizo and rice and cook for 2 minutes, stirring to ensure the chorizo has begun to release its oil and all the rice grains are well coated.

2 Pour the wine into the pan and bring to a simmer, then allow it to bubble down for 1 minute. Pour in the stock, season generously and bring to the boil, then reduce the heat, cover and simmer for 10–12 minutes or until the rice is cooked through and completely tender. Fold in the artichoke hearts and allow to warm through. Season to taste and carefully stir in the parsley. Tip into a warmed serving dish and serve at once.

39 Potato and Carrot Latkes with Spicy Vinaigrette

LESLEY WATERS'S
ACCOMPANIMENT

Serves 2–4

1 large potato, grated

1 large carrot, grated

50 g/2 oz plain flour

1 egg, beaten

5 tbsp milk

5 tbsp olive oil

1 tbsp balsamic vinegar

1 tbsp wholegrain mustard

salt and freshly ground black pepper

fresh whole chives, to garnish (optional)

I love to serve these latkes with sausages or grilled chicken, or with bacon and eggs for a brunch-style breakfast. They would also make a fantastic starter with some lightly dressed salad leaves, and my kids love them with tomato ketchup. The carrot gives them a wonderful colour and surprisingly sweet taste.

1 Dry the grated potato and carrot well on kitchen paper or in a clean tea towel to remove any excess moisture. Place the flour in a large bowl, make a well in the centre and gradually add the egg and milk to form a smooth batter. Season generously and stir in the grated potato and carrot, mixing well to combine.

2 Heat one tablespoon of olive oil in a large non-stick frying pan. Spoon four heaps of the potato and carrot mixture into the pan and press down with the back of the spoon to form four rough, flat rounds. Fry over a medium heat for 4–5 minutes until golden, then flip over and cook for a further 4–5 minutes until cooked through and lightly golden. Keep warm. Repeat with another tablespoon of olive oil and the rest of the potato and carrot mixture to make another four latkes.

3 To make the dressing, place the remaining three tablespoons of olive oil in a small bowl and add the balsamic vinegar and wholegrain mustard. Season to taste, then whisk until well combined and an emulsion has formed. Pile up the latkes on a warm serving dish. Drizzle over the dressing and garnish with the chives, if liked. Serve immediately.

40 Deep-fried Spicy Potato Scallops

TONY TOBIN'S
ACCOMPANIMENT

Serves 2

sunflower oil, for deep-frying

50 g/2 oz plain flour

2 tsp medium curry powder

2 potatoes, cut into 1 cm/^{1}/$_2$ in slices (such as Desirée or King Edward)

salt and freshly ground black pepper

FOR THE BATTER:

115 g/4 oz plain flour

about 175 ml/6 fl oz ice-cold water

These are rather like the battered potato scallops you get in good fish and chip shops in Birmingham, but I've spiced them up. They are excellent served with an aromatic curry or tagine, or they'd make a nice change from poppadums with bowls of chutneys and a raita for dipping. Just don't forget the glasses of ice-cold beer as they are thirsty work …

1 Preheat a deep-fat fryer or a deep-sided pan one-third full of sunflower oil to 190°C/375°F. Place the flour in a bowl and stir in the curry powder, then season generously. To make the batter, place the flour in a bowl with a pinch of salt and then whisk in enough of the water to make a smooth batter with the consistency of single cream. Coat the potato slices in the seasoned flour, shaking off any excess, then quickly dip into the batter.

2 Carefully drop the coated potato slices into the heated oil and deep-fry for 6–8 minutes until crisp and golden brown – you may have to do this in batches depending on the size of your pan. Remove with a slotted spoon and drain on kitchen paper. Pile on to a warmed serving dish and season with salt to serve.

41 Fontina Cheese Scones

ROSS BURDEN'S
ACCOMPANIMENT

Makes 6

115 g/4 oz plain flour, plus extra for dusting

good pinch of salt

1 tsp baking powder

25 g/1 oz unsalted butter

50 g/2 oz Fontina cheese, finely grated

about 85 ml/3 fl oz milk

beaten egg, to glaze (optional)

butter, to serve

Scones remind me of Saturday lunch when I was a student in Auckland. We always made squash soup and scones after the fortnightly shopping expedition. For the best results, cover the cooked scones immediately with a clean tea towel as they cool on the wire rack. This helps them to stay moist and fluffy. Eat within hours, or freeze for up to a month in a rigid plastic container with a lid. To use, defrost at room temperature for 1 hour.

1 Preheat the oven to 220°C/425°F/Gas 7 (fan oven 200°C from cold). Sift the flour, salt and baking powder into a bowl. Rub in the butter and stir in the Fontina cheese, then make a well in the centre and add enough of the milk to quickly mix to a soft dough.

2 Turn the dough out on to a lightly floured surface and knead briefly, then roll out to a 1 cm/½ in thickness. Cut into six rough square shapes and arrange slightly apart on a non-stick baking sheet dusted with flour. Brush the tops with the beaten egg, if liked, and bake for 8–10 minutes until well risen and golden brown.

3 Transfer the cooked scones to a wire rack, cover with a clean tea towel and leave to cool. Arrange in a bread basket and serve with a small pot of butter so that guests can help themselves.

42 Gratin Dauphinois

KEVIN WOODFORD'S
ACCOMPANIMENT

Serves 2

350 g/12 oz Jersey Royal new potatoes, scrubbed

150 ml/¼ pint double cream

50 g/2 oz unsalted butter

1 garlic clove, peeled

salt and freshly ground black pepper

few whole chives, to garnish (optional)

This is comfort cuisine at its best, and one of my favourite accompaniments to enhance any main course, especially lamb or beef. Just look at the ingredients – you know it's got to be good. But stand back from the stove and put down the cream if you are worried about your diet. Personally, I think that a little of everything never did anyone any harm …

1 Preheat the oven to 220°C/425°F/Gas 7 (fan oven 200°C from cold). Thinly slice the potatoes using a mandolin cutter, being very careful of your fingers. Place in a small pan with the cream, 25 g/1 oz of the butter and the garlic. Season generously and bring to the boil, then reduce the heat and simmer for 4 minutes.

2 Generously butter two 10 cm/4 in cooking rings and place on a baking sheet on squares of buttered foil. Remove the potatoes from the cream mixture with a slotted spoon and layer up in the cooking rings, pressing down with the back of a spoon.

3 Spoon a tablespoon or two of remaining cream mixture over each filled cooking ring and dot with the rest of the butter. Bake for 12–15 minutes until the potatoes are cooked through and lightly golden. Remove from the oven and carefully take off the cooking rings, then transfer to warmed serving plates. Garnish with the whole chives, if liked, and serve immediately.

43 Foolproof Yorkshire Puddings

BRIAN TURNER'S
ACCOMPANIMENT

Serves 6–8

115 g/4 oz plain flour

4 eggs (preferably organic or free-range), beaten

200 ml/7 fl oz milk

4 tbsp beef dripping or sunflower oil

salt and freshly ground black pepper

I make these all the time on *Ready Steady Cook* and most of the chefs now follow my example, as there is little doubt that when it comes to Yorkshire puddings these are the best. They are very simple: take equal quantities of flour, eggs and milk – I normally measure in a teacup – and follow the method below for guaranteed excellent results every time. The important thing to remember is to preheat the beef dripping or oil in the tin before pouring in the batter. It needs to be very hot to enable the puddings to rise quickly and to stop them sticking to the moulds.

1 Preheat the oven to 220°C/425°F/Gas 7 (fan oven 200°C from cold). Sift the flour and a pinch of salt into a bowl. Make a well in the centre, then pour in the beaten eggs and gradually draw in the flour. Quickly add the milk and whisk until you have achieved a smooth batter, the consistency of single cream. Season to taste.

2 Place the dripping or oil in two 12-hole bun trays and heat on the top shelf of the oven for 5 minutes. Stir the batter and transfer to a jug, then pour the batter into the hot fat or oil so that it comes halfway up the sides. Bake the Yorkshire puddings for 15–20 minutes until well risen, crisp and golden brown. Pile into a warmed serving dish and serve at once.

44 Tomato and Balsamic Flatbreads

PHIL VICKERY'S
ACCOMPANIMENT

Makes 2

175 g/6 oz self-raising flour, plus extra for dusting

about 5 tbsp milk

2 tbsp thick Greek yoghurt

1 red chilli, seeded and finely chopped

2 tbsp chopped fresh mint

2 tbsp olive oil

12 baby cherry tomatoes

about 1 tbsp balsamic vinegar

salt and freshly ground black pepper

These flatbreads take minutes to prepare as the dough needs to be kneaded very lightly for no more than 30 seconds. Over-kneading will result in a heavy texture after cooking. Once you have mastered the technique, flatbreads can be flavoured with all sorts of variations of herbs and spices. Try chopped fresh coriander with green chilli and turmeric, or crushed cumin seeds and ground paprika with a touch of tomato purée for colour.

1 Heat a large non-stick frying pan and a small sauté pan. Sift the flour into a large bowl with a good pinch of salt. Make a well in the centre and add the five tablespoons of milk with the yoghurt, chilli and mint. Quickly mix to a soft but not sticky dough, adding a little extra milk if necessary.

2 Turn the dough out on to a lightly floured work surface and gently knead to a smooth dough. Divide the dough into two portions and then using a rolling pin roll out each piece of dough to a rough oval shape about 1 cm/$\frac{1}{2}$ in thick.

3 Add a thin film of oil to the large frying pan and cook one of the pieces of dough for 2–3 minutes on each side until cooked through and lightly golden. Remove from the pan, pat dry with kitchen paper and keep warm. Repeat with a little more of the oil and the other piece of dough.

4 Meanwhile, add the remaining olive oil to the small sauté pan. Tip in the cherry tomatoes, tossing to coat in the oil. Sprinkle over the balsamic vinegar and continue to cook for a couple of minutes until the tomatoes begin to burst, tossing the pan occasionally.

5 Season the balsamic tomatoes and spoon on top of the flatbreads. Arrange on a large serving platter or wooden chopping board to serve.

45 Spicy Pinto Bean Cake with Warm Roasted Pepper Salsa

PAUL RANKIN'S
VEGETARIAN RECIPE

Serves 2

¼ tsp each cumin seeds, dried oregano and dried chilli flakes

400 g/14 oz can pinto beans, drained and rinsed

50 g/2 oz plain flour, plus extra for dusting

1 egg white

2 tbsp olive oil

crème fraiche or thick Greek yoghurt, to garnish

FOR THE SALSA:

1 tbsp olive oil

1 red pepper, seeded and finely diced

4 spring onions, thinly sliced

2 ripe tomatoes, seeded and chopped

squeeze of fresh lemon juice

2 tbsp chopped fresh corian-der, plus extra sprigs to garnish

salt and freshly ground black pepper

These tasty bean burgers are miles ahead of any of the shop-bought ones that are now so readily available. Pinto beans are a rich orange-pink with rust-coloured flecks and are traditionally the main ingredient for Mexican refried beans, which is where the idea for this recipe originates. They would also be excellent served in a split ciabatta bun filled with salad.

1 Heat a small frying pan over a low heat and dry-fry the cumin seeds, oregano and chilli flakes for 30 seconds, tossing occasionally, until aromatic.

2 Place the beans in a food processor with the flour and egg white, then pulse until roughly blended. Add the toasted spices and blend briefly to combine – the mixture should still have some texture left and not be completely smooth.

3 Heat two small non-stick frying pans. Season the bean mixture generously, tip out on to a lightly floured board and quickly shape into two patties about 2.5 cm/1 in thick. Add one tablespoon of oil to each pan and fry the bean cakes for 2–3 minutes on each side, until cooked through and golden.

4 Meanwhile, make the salsa. Heat the olive oil in a small pan. Add the pepper and sauté for about 2–3 minutes until just beginning to soften. Add the spring onions and cook for another 2 minutes, stirring, then add the tomatoes, lemon juice and fresh coriander, and continue to cook for 1 minute to warm through. Season.

5 Arrange the pinto bean cakes on warmed serving plates and spoon over the salsa. Using two dessertspoons that have been briefly dipped in boiling water make quenelles of crème fraiche or Greek yoghurt and arrange on top. Garnish with coriander sprigs and serve immediately.

46 Malaysian Sweet Potato Curry

NICK NAIRN'S
VEGETARIAN RECIPE

Serves 4

1 red onion, chopped

1 garlic clove, chopped

1cm/½ in piece of fresh root ginger, chopped

2 red bird's eye chillies, seeded and chopped

1 lemongrass stalk, outer core removed and chopped

2 tbsp ground almonds

2 tbsp sunflower oil

1 tsp each ground cumin, coriander, paprika and turmeric

500 g/1 lb 2 oz sweet potatoes, cut into 1 cm/½ in chunks

300 ml/½ pint vegetable stock

400 g/14 oz can coconut milk

juice of 1 lime

salt and freshly ground black pepper

steamed basmati rice, to serve

chopped fresh coriander, to garnish

This recipe I devised on *Ready Steady Cook* is now my favourite vegetable curry which I make all the time. That's proof that dishes taste as good as they look on the show. It makes a very hot curry, but feel free to add as little chilli – or as much – as you desire. Puréeing the onions before cooking is a popular Malay technique that gives a distinctive texture to the curry, helped by the addition of the almonds, a natural thickener.

1 Place the onion in a mini food processor with the garlic, ginger, chillies, lemongrass, almonds, oil and spices. Whizz until well combined to a purée.

2 Heat a large pan. Add the onion paste and stir-fry for 2–3 minutes until cooked through but not coloured. Add the sweet potatoes and continue to stir-fry for another 2–3 minutes until just beginning to colour. Season generously.

3 Pour the vegetable stock into the pan with the coconut milk, stirring to combine. Bring to the boil, then reduce the heat and simmer for 15 minutes or until the sweet potatoes are completely tender but still holding their shape.

4 Stir the lime juice into the sweet potato curry and season to taste. Divide the rice among warmed serving bowls and ladle in the curry. Garnish with the coriander leaves and serve at once.

47 Spinach Roulade with Feta and Sun-blushed Tomatoes

AINSLEY HARRIOTT'S
VEGETARIAN RECIPE

Serves 4

50 g/2 oz unsalted butter, plus extra for greasing

40 g/1½ oz plain flour

300 ml/½ pint milk

250 g/9 oz tender young spinach leaves

3 eggs (preferably organic or free-range)

50 g/2 oz pine nuts

150 g/5 oz feta cheese

2 tbsp chopped fresh flat-leaf parsley

6 sun-blushed tomatoes, chopped

salt and freshly cracked black pepper

lightly dressed mixed leaf salad, to serve

I know this dish sounds like a culinary cliché, but well done the results can be spectacular and impress vegetarians and carnivores alike. The warmth of the soufflé marries the filling flavours together and softens the feta cheese slightly. Experiment with the filling; I particularly like Stilton, walnut and chopped fresh flat-leaf parsley, or plenty of thinly sliced smoked salmon arranged on a layer of cream cheese.

1 Preheat the oven to 200°C/400°F/Gas 6 (fan oven 180°C from cold). Grease and line a Swiss-roll tin with non-stick baking paper. Melt 40 g/1½ oz of the butter in a pan, then stir in the flour and cook for 1 minute. Gradually add the milk, stirring until smooth after each addition. Remove from the heat, then using a spatula transfer to a large bowl and allow to cool a little.

2 Heat the remaining knob of butter in a pan, add the spinach and stir-fry for a minute or so until just wilted. Drain and squeeze out the excess moisture, then finely chop. Separate the eggs and whisk the whites in a bowl until stiff. Stir the egg yolks into the white sauce with the finely chopped spinach, then season to taste. Gently fold in the egg whites and carefully pour into the prepared tin. Bake for 12–15 minutes or until well risen and firm to the touch. Turn out on to a wire rack, peel off the paper and allow to cool a little.

3 Toast the pine nuts in a small frying pan, then place in a bowl and crumble in the feta and add the parsley and sun-blushed tomatoes. Season with pepper and stir gently to combine, then scatter over the roulade. Trim the edges with a sharp knife and then roll up to enclose the filling. Cut into slices and arrange on serving plates with some of the salad alongside.

48 Courgette and Parmesan Frittata

ANTONY WORRALL
THOMPSON'S VEGETARIAN
RECIPE

Serves 4

4 tbsp extra virgin olive oil

1 onion, thinly sliced

**2 courgettes, finely sliced
(about 350 g/12 oz in total)**

1 tsp fresh thyme leaves

3 garlic cloves, crushed

**6 large eggs (preferably
organic or free-range)**

**85 g/3 oz freshly grated
Parmesan**

2 tbsp torn fresh basil leaves

**salt and freshly ground black
pepper**

**lightly dressed sun-dried
tomato and baby green leaf
salad, to serve (optional)**

Nowadays we take courgettes for granted, but it's not so long ago that they were a luxury vegetable. Everybody tends to serve them very crunchy – al dente – which is great, but they produce a wonderful frittata when cooked a little longer with extra virgin olive oil. Frittatas are thick omelettes cooked until firm. They make the ultimate picnic food, especially since they taste just as good cold as hot or warm.

1 Preheat the oven to 180°C/350°F/Gas 4 (fan oven 160°C from cold). Heat half the oil in a heavy-based ovenproof pan about 23 cm/9 in diameter. Add the onion and cook for 2–3 minutes until softened but not browned, stirring frequently. Stir in the courgettes, thyme and garlic and cook for another 4–5 minutes until softened, stirring occasionally. Season to taste.

2 Meanwhile, break the eggs into a large bowl and lightly beat to combine. Add half of the Parmesan and the basil and beat in to combine. When the courgettes are cooked, stir them into the egg mixture and season to taste. Heat the remaining oil in the frying pan, swirling to coat the sides evenly. Pour in the courgette and egg mixture and cook for 2–3 minutes over a low heat to set the bottom and sides.

3 Scatter the remaining Parmesan on top of the frittata, transfer the pan to the oven and cook, uncovered, for another 10 minutes until just set, puffed up and lightly golden. Loosen the sides with a palette knife and turn out on to a large, warmed serving plate. Serve warm or at room temperature, cut into wedges, with a big bowl of salad, if liked.

49 Lemon and Parmesan Risotto with Sugar-roasted Tomatoes

LESLEY WATERS'S
VEGETARIAN RECIPE

Serves 4

2 tbsp olive oil

1 onion, chopped

1 lemon

350 g/12oz Arborio (risotto) rice

8 tomatoes on the vine

1 tsp sugar

about 900 ml/1½ pints vegetable stock

300 ml/½ pint white wine

25 g/1 oz unsalted butter

50 g/2 oz freshly grated Parmesan

25 g/1 oz wild rocket leaves

salt and freshly ground black pepper

The secret of a good risotto is to start by using a good quality heavy-based, shallow pan – a sauté pan is perfect. Use a speciality risotto rice, such as Arborio, which can absorb up to six times its volume in liquid, and most importantly add the hot stock little by little, allowing each ladleful to be completely absorbed before adding the next. Follow these simple rules and you achieve perfect results every time – I promise!

1 Preheat the oven to 200°C/400°F/Gas 6 (fan oven 180°C from cold). Heat one tablespoon of the oil in a large, shallow pan. Add the onion and cook gently for 10 minutes until softened but not coloured. Pare one large curl of rind from the lemon and stir it into the pan with the rice. Cook gently for 2–3 minutes, stirring, until the rice is opaque.

2 Place the tomatoes on the vine in a small baking tin. Drizzle over the remaining tablespoon of olive oil and sprinkle the sugar on top. Roast for 12–15 minutes until lightly charred and softened, but still holding their shape.

3 Meanwhile, pour the vegetable stock into a pan and bring to a gentle simmer. Pour the wine into the rice mixture and allow it to reduce, stirring until it is completely absorbed. Begin to add the simmering stock a ladleful at a time, stirring frequently. Allow each stock addition to be absorbed before adding the next.

4 After about 20 minutes, the rice should be just tender but still have a little bite – al dente. Remove the lemon rind from the risotto and stir in the butter. Cut the lemon in half and add a good squeeze of juice to the risotto, then season to taste and add the Parmesan, stirring energetically to combine. Ladle into a large serving dish and arrange the sugar-roasted tomatoes on top with the rocket. Serve at once.

50 Wild Mushroom and Leek Cannelloni

TONY TOBIN'S
VEGETARIAN RECIPE

Serves 2

3 egg yolks

115 g/4 oz plain flour, plus extra for dusting

2 tbsp olive oil

1 small onion, finely chopped

2 leeks, sliced on the diagonal

350 g/12 oz mixed wild mushrooms, sliced (such as chanterelle, cep, shiitake, oyster and chestnut)

120 ml/4 fl oz dry white wine

225 ml/8 fl oz double cream

1 tsp Dijon mustard

50 g/2 oz freshly grated Parmesan

salt and freshly ground black pepper

lightly dressed mixed leaf salad, to serve (optional)

I often make my own pasta on the show – once you've mastered the technique it really is easy. In the restaurant I like to use type '00' pasta flour and semolina flour for dusting, but ordinary plain flour achieves pretty decent results. Alternatively, start with six shop-bought fresh lasagne sheets and you are halfway there.

1 Preheat the oven to 200°C/400°F/Gas 6 (fan oven 180°C from cold) and preheat the grill to medium. To make the pasta, place two of the egg yolks and a pinch of salt in a food processor, then with the motor running add the flour, tablespoon by tablespoon, through the feeder tube until the mixture resembles fine breadcrumbs. Tip out on to a lightly floured work surface and squeeze the mixture together to form a ball, then divide into six balls. Wrap in clingfilm and chill for at least 5 minutes (or up to 2 hours if time allows).

2 Roll out the dough a piece at a time using a pasta machine, dusting with flour as you go. Pass through the widest setting three times, then gradually narrow the setting as you roll out until you have a thin, pliable pasta sheet, finally passing through the thinnest setting three times. Trim down to a square of about 10x15 cm/4x6 in. Repeat, covering the pasta with a damp cloth, until you have six in total.

3 Meanwhile, heat the oil in a frying pan and fry the onion and leeks for 1–2 minutes until just beginning to soften. Stir in the mushrooms, season and cook for another 3–4 minutes until the mushrooms are tender, stirring occasionally. Pour in the wine and allow it to bubble down, then pour in 150 ml/$1/4$ pint of the cream and add the mustard. Cook for a minute or two until slightly reduced and thickened, stirring. Season to taste, then transfer to a bowl to cool down slightly.

4 Blanch the pasta sheets briefly in a pan of boiling salted water, then plunge into a bowl of ice-cold water and drain. Pat dry with kitchen paper. Lightly butter an ovenproof dish. Spoon some of the mushroom and leek mixture into each lasagne sheet and carefully roll up to enclose. Arrange in the buttered dish.

5 Mix the rest of the cream in a small bowl with the remaining egg yolk and half of the Parmesan. Spoon over the cannelloni and scatter the rest of the Parmesan on top. Bake for 5–10 minutes until heated through, then flash under the hot grill until lightly golden. Serve straight from the dish with a bowl of the salad, if liked.

51 Gnocchi with Sage Butter

KEVIN WOODFORD'S
VEGETARIAN RECIPE

Serves 2

450 g/1 lb potatoes, chopped

good pinch of salt

50 g/2 oz plain flour, plus extra for dusting

85 g/3 oz unsalted butter

handful of chopped fresh sage leaves

freshly grated Parmesan, to serve (optional)

When Fiona Phillips came on *Celebrity Ready Steady Cook* and tipped out her bag I couldn't believe my eyes. All she had brought was a huge bag of potatoes and absolutely nothing else. I had a momentary panic before realizing that there was quite a bit I could make with them and ingredients from the larder. This, however, was her favourite dish so I had to include it, and it is now also a firm favourite among my vegetarian friends.

1 Place the potatoes in a pan of boiling salted water, cover and simmer for 10–12 minutes until completely tender. Drain and return to the pan for a couple of seconds to dry out. With a wooden spoon, push the potatoes through a sieve set over a bowl. Add the salt, flour and 25 g/1 oz of the butter, then mix briefly to bind.

2 Place a large pan of boiling salted water on to simmer. Using floured hands, turn the potato mixture out on to a lightly floured work surface and knead lightly until soft and smooth. Gently roll the dough into a long sausage shape about 2.5 cm/1 in in diameter. Cut into 2 cm/³⁄₄ in pieces, then quickly roll each piece over the end of the prongs of a fork to mark grooves. Dust in flour.

3 Add the gnocchi to the pan of simmering water a few at a time and cook gently for 2–3 minutes or until the gnocchi float to the surface. Remove with a slotted spoon and transfer to a warm serving dish.

4 Meanwhile, melt the remaining butter in a small pan with the sage leaves and cook over a very gentle heat to allow the flavours to infuse for a couple of minutes. Pour over the gnocchi and scatter over the Parmesan to serve, if you've got it (unfortunately, I didn't!).

52 Asparagus Cream Pasta

PHIL VICKERY'S VEGETARIAN
RECIPE

Serves 2

**115 g/4 oz fine asparagus
spears**

25 g/1 oz unsalted butter

4 spring onions, finely chopped

1 tbsp dry white wine

150 ml/¼ pint double cream

2 tsp wholegrain mustard

3 tbsp snipped fresh chives

**225 g/8 oz fresh tagliatelle
pasta**

**salt and freshly ground black
pepper**

**freshly grated Parmesan, to
garnish (optional)**

Supermarkets now offer an incredible selection of freshly prepared pasta, while traditional Italian delis can stock up to a dozen different varieties. Unfortunately, fresh does not always mean best and I have on occasion been disappointed with the quality of the pasta sold in supermarkets – it lacks bite when cooked. Look out for pasta made from durum wheat semolina.

1 Cut the asparagus into 4 cm/1½ in lengths. Plunge the stems into a pan of boiling salted water and simmer for 1 minute, then add the tips and cook for another 1 minute or so until just tender. Drain and quickly refresh under cold running water. Set aside.

2 Melt the butter in a frying pan and add the spring onions. Sauté for 30 seconds, then sprinkle over the wine and pour in the cream. Increase the heat, season to taste and simmer for 2–3 minutes or until slightly reduced and thickened. Stir the mustard into the pan with the chives and blanched asparagus. Allow to warm through, stirring.

3 Meanwhile, bring a large pan of water to a rolling boil. Add the pasta, stir once and simmer for 1–2 minutes or according to packet instructions. Drain the pasta and quickly refresh under cold running water. Return to the pan and stir in the asparagus cream. Season to taste and divide between warmed wide-rimmed bowls. Scatter over the Parmesan, to garnish, if liked. Serve immediately.

Vegetarian

53 Bubble and Squeak with Fried Eggs

BRIAN TURNER'S
VEGETARIAN RECIPE

Serves 2

450 g/1 lb floury potatoes, cut into 2.5 cm/1 in cubes (Golden Wonder, King Edward or Maris Piper)

115 g/4 oz Savoy or York cabbage, roughly chopped

85 g/3 oz unsalted butter

2 tbsp milk

2 tbsp sunflower oil

4 large eggs (preferably organic or free-range, and as fresh as possible)

salt and freshly ground black pepper

I have been taking part in *Ready Steady Cook* ever since the show started in October 1994 and, as many of you know, vegetarian dishes are not my forte. However, bubble and squeak is an old-fashioned favourite of mine and my dad's that just happens not to have meat in it. Comforting yet homely, this classic leftover recipe for greens is lovely served with fried eggs, and you don't even have to wait for leftovers to make it. If you are not a vegetarian, or find yourself catering for both, serve it with sausages or slices of cooked ham and turkey with a selection of pickles …

1 Place the potatoes in a large pan of boiling salted water. Bring to the boil, cover and simmer for 8–10 minutes until tender but not breaking up. Plunge the cabbage into a pan of boiling salted water and cook for 6–8 minutes until tender. Drain and quickly refresh under cold running water.

2 Heat a large non-stick frying pan. Drain the potatoes and return to their pan over a low heat to dry out. Mash them, then beat in half of the butter and the milk. Season to taste and finally fold in the cooked cabbage.

3 Add half of the oil and a knob of the butter to the frying pan and swirl it up the sides. Tip in the potato mixture and cook for about 10 minutes, turning over regularly so the crispy brown underside gets folded through.

4 Heat an omelette pan and add half the remaining oil and butter. Break two eggs into the pan and use a metal spoon to baste for a minute or so until just set. Divide the bubble and squeak between two warmed serving plates and slide the fried eggs on top of one serving. Keep warm. Heat the rest of the oil and butter in the pan and cook the remaining eggs. Slide on the second portion of bubble and squeak and serve at once.

54 Tomato and Goats' Cheese Tart with Pesto

JAMES MARTIN'S
VEGETARIAN RECIPE

Serves 2

small goats' cheese, rind on
(about 115 g/4 oz)

about 6 tbsp olive oil

1 tsp fresh thyme leaves

knob of unsalted butter

1 small red onion, thinly sliced

200 g/7 oz cherry tomatoes

1 tsp sugar

2 tbsp balsamic vinegar

50 g/2oz fresh basil leaves

1 small garlic clove, peeled

1 tbsp toasted pine nuts

fresh chervil, basil and flat-leaf
parsley salad, to garnish

FOR THE PASTRY:

200 g/7 oz plain flour, plus
extra for dusting

115 g/4 oz unsalted butter,
chilled and diced

1 egg (preferably organic or
free-range)

pinch of salt

1–2 tbsp ice-cold water

salt and freshly ground black
pepper

This is a classic flavour combination. The sharp flavour of the goats' cheese complements the sweet and sour sautéed tomatoes, while the basil pesto cuts through the creaminess of the cheese. Try to get a young Sainte-Maure or Crottin de Chavignol, or the English Chabis. Some of the more mature goat's cheeses tend to be crumbly inside, with a concentrated chalky flavour that not everybody likes.

1 Preheat the oven to 220°C/425°F/Gas 7 (fan oven 200°C from cold). Blitz the ingredients for the pastry in a food processor, adding just enough of the ice-cold water to make a soft dough. Roll out thinly on a lightly floured surface and cut out two circles roughly 10 cm/4 in in diameter. Transfer to a non-stick baking sheet. Prick each pastry circle all over with a fork and bake for 8 minutes until cooked through and lightly golden.

2 Split the goat's cheese in half around the equator and place in a small baking dish. Brush with a little of the oil and sprinkle with the thyme leaves. Season and bake for 4–5 minutes until bubbling but still holding their shape.

3 Melt the knob of butter in a frying pan with a little oil, then add the onion. Cook for 1–2 minutes until just beginning to soften, stirring. Tip in the tomatoes and cook over a high heat for 2–3 minutes, then sprinkle over the sugar and then the vinegar, allowing it to bubble down. Season, reduce the heat and continue to cook for another couple of minutes until the tomatoes begin to split.

4 To make the pesto, place the basil leaves in a mini food processor with the garlic, pine nuts and remaining four tablespoons of olive oil. Blend until you have achieved a smooth purée, then season to taste and pour into a small jug, whisking in a little more oil if the pesto seems too thick.

5 Remove the pastry bases from the oven and carefully slide on to warmed serving plates. Pile the tomato mixture on to each pastry disc and place a piece of the bubbling goat's cheese on top. Drizzle over the pesto and garnish with a small mound of the herb salad. Serve immediately.

55 Broccoli and Feta Pancakes with Tomato Sauce

ROSS BURDEN'S
VEGETARIAN RECIPE

Serves 4

150 g/5 oz plain flour

2 eggs (preferably organic or free-range)

about 300 ml/½ pint milk

2 tbsp snipped fresh chives

olive oil, for frying

about 50 g/2 oz unsalted butter

1 small red onion

1 garlic clove, crushed

400 g/14 oz can chopped tomatoes (in rich tomato juice)

2 tsp tomato purée

350 g/12 oz broccoli, cut into small florets

115 g/4 oz feta cheese

85 g/3 oz black olives, pitted

2 tbsp chopped mixed fresh herbs (such as flat-leaf parsley and basil)

salt and freshly ground black pepper

lightly dressed mixed salad, to serve

Canned tomatoes make surprisingly fresh-tasting sauces, especially if you add a handful of fresh herbs and some garlic. Please try to use black olives that you pit yourself – they often sell them in supermarkets – which are actually green olives dyed black.

1 To make the pancake batter, sift the flour and a pinch of salt into a bowl, then make a well in the centre. Break in the eggs and add a little of the milk. Mix the liquid ingredients together, then gradually take in the flour and beat until smooth. Finally beat in the remaining milk until you have a batter the consistency of single cream. Stir in the chives and leave to rest for 5 minutes (or up to 30 minutes covered with clingfilm in the fridge if time allows).

2 Heat a large non-stick pan and, when hot, brush with the minimum of oil and add a little of the butter. Pour a small amount of the batter into the pan and swirl it around until it evenly covers the bottom. Cook for 1 minute until the edges are curling away from the pan and the underside is golden. Flip over and cook for another minute or so. Transfer the pancake to a plate lined with a square of non-stick baking paper. Repeat until you have eight pancakes in total, layering them up on the plate between squares of the non-stick baking paper.

3 Meanwhile, make the tomato sauce. Heat a tablespoon of oil in a frying pan. Add the onion and cook for 2–3 minutes until softened and not coloured, stirring. Stir in the garlic and cook for 30 seconds or so, then add the tomatoes and tomato purée. Season to taste. Bring to the boil, then reduce the heat and simmer for 8–10 minutes until slightly reduced and thickened, stirring from time to time.

4 Cook the broccoli in a pan of boiling salted water for 2–3 minutes until tender. Drain and quickly refresh under cold running water. Place in a large bowl and crumble in the feta. Stir in the olives and herbs, then fold in the tomato sauce. Season to taste.

5 Divide the broccoli mixture between the pancakes. Roll up to enclose the filling and then arrange in a single layer, seam-side down, in a lightly buttered oven-proof dish. Dot with the remaining butter and bake for about 5 minutes until the pancakes are heated through. Serve the pancakes straight from the dish with a large bowl of salad alongside.

56 Cajun-style Salmon with Hot Relish and Courgette Chips

PHIL VICKERY'S FISH AND SHELLFISH RECIPE

Serves 2

sunflower oil, for deep-frying

1 tsp each ground cumin, coriander, mixed spice and dried oregano

2 x 115 g/4 oz salmon fillets, scaled and boned

2 tbsp olive oil

1 red onion, finely diced

10 cherry tomatoes, finely diced

1 tsp dried chilli flakes

1 tbsp dry white wine

juice of 1 lime

2 tsp caster sugar

handful of chopped fresh coriander

2 large courgettes, trimmed, halved and cut into sticks

50 g/2 oz seasoned flour

2 eggs (preferably organic or free-range)

salt and freshly ground black pepper

thick soured cream, to garnish

I just love fishing and try to make time for it whenever I can. A number of years ago I went to Australia and New Zealand for an extended holiday and managed to catch my largest salmon ever – a fraction over 25 pounds in weight. This recipe is based on what I did with that fish. On the barbecue it tasted wonderful, slightly blackened but still moist and tender in the centre – delicious.

1 Preheat a deep-fat fryer or a deep-sided pan one-third full of sunflower oil to 190°C/375°F, and preheat a non-stick heavy-based frying pan. Mix the spices and oregano in a shallow dish. Season and use to coat the flesh-side of each salmon fillet. Add one tablespoon of the oil to the heated frying pan and then add the salmon fillets, skin-side down. Cook for 3–4 minutes until the skin is crisp and golden, then turn over and cook for another couple of minutes until lightly seared.

2 Meanwhile, make the hot tomato relish. Heat the remaining tablespoon of olive oil in a frying pan. Add the onions and sauté for 2–3 minutes until softened but not coloured, stirring occasionally. Add the tomatoes and chilli flakes, then simmer for 2 minutes. Sprinkle over the wine, lime juice and sugar, then stir well to combine and allow the sugar to melt. Tip in the coriander, season to taste and keep warm.

3 To prepare the courgette chips, first place the flour in one bowl and beat the eggs with a little seasoning in another. Dip the courgette sticks into the egg and then toss in the flour to coat, shaking off any excess. Deep-fry for 2–3 minutes or until crisp and golden brown – you may have to do this in batches. Drain well on kitchen paper and arrange in the middle of warmed serving plates. Top each one with Cajun-style salmon fillets and garnish with a spoonful of soured cream. Spoon around the hot relish to serve.

57 Chargrilled Salmon with Couscous Salad and Sauce Vierge

NICK NAIRN'S FISH AND
SHELLFISH RECIPE

Serves 2

1 red and 1 yellow pepper, halved, seeded and cut into eighths

1 courgette, cut into slices on the diagonal

85 ml/3 fl oz extra virgin olive oil, plus extra for brushing

2 spring onions, finely chopped

1 garlic clove, lightly crushed

115 g/4 oz couscous

150 ml/¼ pint vegetable stock

4 tbsp roughly chopped fresh basil

juice of 1 lemon

2 x 150 g/5 oz salmon fillets

2 ripe plum tomatoes, peeled, seeded and chopped

sea salt and freshly ground black pepper

This dish is a great dinner-party staple. Most of the work can be done well in advance and it looks and tastes fantastic. I'm a big fan of farmed salmon and in my opinion some of the best available in this country comes from Shetland, which has freezing cold, unpolluted waters with strong tidal flows. When chargrilling the salmon and vegetables, don't be tempted to fiddle with them: you want to get nice dark griddle lines. This also helps to caramelize the salmon's juices and produces a tastier fillet.

1 Heat a griddle pan until searing hot. Brush all the pepper pieces and courgette slices with some of the olive oil and add to the griddle pan in batches. Chargrill for about 5 minutes on each side until tender and nicely marked. Place in a shallow dish, season generously and set aside to cool a little.

2 To prepare the sauce vierge, place four tablespoons of the olive oil in a small pan with the spring onions and garlic. Warm through for 5 minutes over a gentle heat until the sauce is hot, but not boiling – you want to soften not colour them.

3 Meanwhile, make the couscous. Heat the stock in a small pan to a gentle simmer, then place the couscous in a bowl and pour the hot stock over. Cover with clingfilm and set aside for 5 minutes, then remove the clingfilm and, using a fork, fluff up the grains so that they separate. Dice the chargrilled vegetables and stir into the couscous with half of the basil, the remaining three tablespoons of olive oil and half the lemon juice. Season to taste.

4 Reheat the griddle pan and brush with a little oil. Season the salmon fillets and chargrill for 2–3 minutes on each side. To finish the sauce, lift out the garlic and discard, then stir in the remaining basil and lemon juice with the tomatoes. Allow to warm through. Divide the couscous between serving plates and top each one with a salmon fillet. Spoon around the sauce vierge to serve.

58 Crispy Fried Sole with Green Beans and Aïoli

PAUL RANKIN'S FISH AND SHELLFISH RECIPE

Serves 2

sunflower oil, for deep-frying

2 egg yolks

2 tsp Dijon mustard

3 garlic cloves, crushed

1 tsp white wine vinegar

100 ml/3½ fl oz sunflower oil

100 ml/3½ fl oz olive oil, plus a little extra

115 g/4 oz fine green beans, trimmed

1 egg white

2 tbsp double cream

4 lemon sole fillets, skinned

50 g/2 oz plain flour

salt and freshly ground black pepper

fresh whole chives, to garnish

People love this dish. It's so easy to make, versatile and satisfying. Serve the crispy fried sole with absolutely anything, from salad to stir-fried vegetables or spicy shoestring chips. The technique works with any type of sole that's available, or try skate wings cut into 2.5 cm/1 in pieces.

1 Preheat a deep-fat fryer or a deep-sided pan one-third full of sunflower oil to 180°C/350°F. To make the aïoli, beat the egg yolks in a small bowl with the mustard, garlic, vinegar, one tablespoon of water and seasoning, until thickened.

2 Mix the oils together in a jug and then begin to add to the egg-yolk mixture, drop by drop, whisking constantly. After adding two tablespoons of oil the mixture should be quite thick. Add the remaining oil more quickly, a teaspoon at a time, whisking constantly. Season to taste, then transfer to a plastic squeezy bottle (or bowl covered with clingfilm) and chill until ready to use.

3 Blanch the beans in a pan of boiling salted water for 3–4 minutes until they are cooked but still a bit crunchy. Drain well and refresh under cold running water. Return half to the pan and set aside, then very finely slice the other half (as fine as if you were cutting chives) and place in a bowl.

4 Add the egg white to the bowl of finely chopped beans and then whisk in the cream until well combined. Pat the sole fillets dry with kitchen paper and cut each one in half on the slight diagonal. Add to the egg white mixture and rub in well to ensure each piece has a good coating.

5 Tip the flour on to a flat plate and season generously, then gently massage into each piece of sole, patting it well to coat evenly. Carefully drop into the heated oil and deep-fry for 2–3 minutes until crisp and golden brown – you may have to do this in batches depending on the size of your pan. Drain on kitchen paper. Add a little olive oil to the reserved beans and quickly reheat, then arrange on warmed serving plates and pile the crispy fried sole on top. Drizzle around the aïoli and garnish with chives to serve.

59 Herb-crusted Cod with Pak Choi and Poached Tomatoes

TONY TOBIN'S FISH AND
SHELLFISH RECIPE

Serves 4

225 g/8 oz pomodorino
tomatoes (baby plum)

200 ml/7 fl oz red wine

2 tbsp red wine vinegar

1 tbsp caster sugar

handful of fresh basil leaves

1 small bunch of fresh flat-leaf
parsley

1 small bunch of fresh chives

4 slices white bread, crusts
removed, cut into cubes

about 4 tbsp olive oil

4 x 150 g/5 oz cod fillets,
skinned and boned

2 small pak choi

salt and freshly ground black
pepper

This simple dish is a masterpiece – no one will ever know you haven't been slaving away in the kitchen for hours. Make sure you use a thick coating of crumbs on each portion of fish so that when it's cooked the cod has a delicious crunchy crust. If cod is unavailable, any firm-fleshed fish would make a good substitute, such as haddock, hake or even salmon.

1 Preheat the oven to 220°C/425°F/Gas 7 (fan oven 200°C from cold). To poach the tomatoes, bring the wine and vinegar to a gentle simmer in a pan. Stir in the sugar until dissolved, then tip in the tomatoes and cook gently for a couple of minutes until the skins have all begun to burst. Remove with a slotted spoon and peel away the skins. Return the tomatoes to the pan with the basil and leave to cool completely (up to 24 hours is best).

2 Remove the leaves from the parsley and discard the stalks, then place in a food processor with the chives and bread cubes. Blend until you have achieved fine breadcrumbs. Tip into a bowl and stir in about two teaspoons of the oil, then season. Season the cod fillets and spread the herb crumb mixture evenly on top, pressing it down firmly to ensure it sticks.

3 Heat a large ovenproof frying pan and add a thin film of oil to the base. Fry the cod fillets crumb-side up for 1 minute to seal, then transfer to the oven and bake for 6–8 minutes or until the cod is tender and the crust is lightly golden.

4 Separate the pak choi leaves, then steam them over a pan of simmering water for 2–3 minutes until wilted. Arrange on warmed serving plates and place a herb-crusted cod fillet on top of each one. Reheat the tomatoes in the wine mixture, then remove with a slotted spoon and drain on kitchen paper. Scatter around the plates and then drizzle each plate with a little of the remaining olive oil. Season with pepper and serve immediately.

60 Monkfish Skewers with Asparagus Pesto

ANTONY WORRALL
THOMPSON'S FISH AND
SHELLFISH RECIPE

Serves 2

350 g/12 oz piece of monkfish tail, well trimmed

1 tsp cumin seeds

1 tsp medium curry powder

$\frac{1}{4}$ tsp cayenne pepper

1 tsp ground turmeric

150 g/5 oz Thai jasmine rice

5 lemongrass stalks

50 g/2 oz fine asparagus spears

1 garlic clove, chopped

5 cm/2 in piece of galangal, peeled and cut into thin slices

1 green chilli, seeded

3 tbsp chopped mixed fresh coriander, chives and parsley

about 8 tbsp olive oil

8 fresh kaffir lime leaves (optional)

salt and freshly ground black pepper

This Asian-inspired asparagus pesto makes a nice change. I am using it here as a dipping sauce for the monkfish kebabs but it would also be fantastic folded into pasta, noodles or rice, or try stuffing it underneath the skin of a chicken breast before cooking.

1 To marinate the monkfish, place the cumin seeds in a small heated frying pan and toast for 30 seconds to 1 minute. Transfer to a mini blender or food processor and add the curry powder, cayenne pepper and half of the turmeric. Season to taste and whizz to a fine powder. Cut the monkfish into bite-sized pieces – you'll need 12 in total – and place in a shallow non-metallic dish. Tip in the spice mixture and toss until the fish is thoroughly coated. Cover with clingfilm and chill to allow the flavours to develop for 10 minutes (or up to 30 minutes if time allows).

2 Meanwhile, tip the Thai jasmine rice into a pan with a tight-fitting lid. Cover with 2.5 cm/1 in of water and add a good pinch of salt and the remaining turmeric. Trim the lemongrass stalks and then finely chop one of the stalks and add to the rice, reserving the rest to use for the kebabs. Cover the pan and bring to a rolling boil for 30 seconds, then reduce the heat and simmer gently for 10 minutes. Remove from the heat and set aside for 5 minutes without lifting the lid.

3 To make the Asian asparagus pesto, chop the asparagus spears into 4 cm/1$\frac{1}{2}$ in lengths. Plunge the stalks into a pan of boiling water, then leave to cook for 3–4 minutes. Add the tips and cook for another 2 minutes then drain and rinse well under cold running water. Reserve some of the asparagus tips for garnish. Place the garlic in a food processor with half of the galangal, the green chilli and herbs. Season to taste and whizz until blended, pouring in enough of the oil through the feeder tube to make a smooth purée. Add the asparagus and blend again briefly.

4 Preheat a heavy-based griddle pan over a medium heat until searing hot. Thread the marinated monkfish on to the reserved lemongrass stalks, alternating with kaffir lime leaves, if using, and the remaining slices of galangal. Brush the griddle pan with the remaining oil and cook the kebabs for 30 seconds to 1 minute on each side until just tender but lightly charred. Stir the cooked rice with a fork to gently fluff up the grains and spoon on to warmed serving plates. Pour the asparagus pesto into dipping bowls and place to the side. Arrange the kebabs on top of the rice and garnish with reserved asparagus spears. Serve at once.

61 Tataki Tuna on Rice Salad with Coconut Dressing

ROSS BURDEN'S FISH AND
SHELLFISH RECIPE

Serves 2

175 g/6 oz basmati rice

4 spring onions, trimmed

120 ml/4 fl oz coconut milk

juice of $\frac{1}{2}$ lime

$\frac{1}{4}$ tsp dried chilli flakes

50 g/2 oz sesame seeds

2 x 150 g/5 oz tuna steaks, at least 2.5 cm/1 in thick

sunflower oil, for brushing

salt and freshly ground black pepper

dark soy sauce, to serve

The idea of this dish is that the tuna is cooked in the pan so briefly that only the outside is coloured and caramelized, and the sesame seeds make a crunchy toasted coating, while the inside is practically raw. Try to remove the tuna from the fridge 15 minutes ahead of cooking so it is not still cold in the middle after being seared. If you keep the portion size down, this also makes an exquisite starter.

1 Bring a large, tight-lidded pan of salted water to the boil. Wash the rice under the tap until the water runs clear. Add the rice to the pan, stir once and cook for 8 minutes. Drain well, return to the pan and cover with the lid. Set aside for another 8–10 minutes and allow the rice to finish cooking in its own steam.

2 Finely shred the spring onions and place in a bowl half filled with ice and topped up with cold water. Set aside and allow to curl. To prepare the dressing, place the coconut milk in a small bowl and whisk in the lime juice and chilli flakes. Season to taste, then set aside.

3 Heat a heavy-based non-stick frying pan. Tip the sesame seeds on to a plate and season generously. Brush the tuna with a little oil and then press into the sesame seed mixture to coat. Cook the tuna for 1 minute on each side until lightly seared on the outside but still raw in the centre. Remove from the pan on to a warmed plate and leave to rest for a minute or so, then, using a very sharp knife, cut into 5 mm/$\frac{1}{4}$ in slices.

4 Drain the spring onions and pat dry on kitchen paper, then fold into the rice with the coconut dressing. Spoon on to warmed serving plates and arrange slices of the tuna on top in a slightly overlapping layer. Serve at once with separate tiny bowls of soy sauce for dipping.

62 Spicy Mackerel Fillets with Fruity Tomato Chutney

BRIAN TURNER'S FISH AND SHELLFISH RECIPE

Serves 2

2 tbsp olive oil

1 small onion, finely chopped

1 garlic clove, crushed

1 large apple, peeled, cored and chopped

2 plum tomatoes, peeled, seeded and chopped

1 tsp balsamic vinegar

1 tbsp dark muscovado sugar

about 4 tbsp plain flour

$^1/_2$ tsp each ground paprika, cayenne pepper and garam masala

2 fresh mackerel, filleted and boned

50 g/2 oz unsalted butter

250 g/9 oz fresh spinach leaves

$^1/_2$ lemon, pips removed

salt and freshly ground black pepper

Mackerel is one of my favourite fish for pan-frying. It cooks firm and succulent, has excellent flavour and is quite a bit cheaper than cod or haddock. When buying mackerel, freshness is the most important quality to look for, so buy from a reliable fishmonger. As it is quite an oily fish it tastes best on the day it was caught. If you are lucky enough to get it spanking fresh, I promise you'll understand what all the fuss is about.

1 To make the chutney, heat one tablespoon of the oil in a pan and add the onion, garlic, apple and tomatoes. Cook for 5 minutes or until the mixture has started to soften, stirring occasionally. Add the vinegar and sugar and continue to cook for another 10–12 minutes, stirring occasionally until the whole mixture has reduced and thickened. Season to taste.

2 Heat a large frying pan. Mix together the flour and spices on a flat plate. Season generously and use to coat the mackerel fillets, shaking off any excess. Add the remaining oil and a knob of butter to the pan and add the fillets skin-side down. Fry over a medium-high heat for 2–3 minutes until the skin is crisp and lightly golden, then turn over and cook for another minute or two until the mackerel fillets are just tender, being careful not to overcook.

3 Heat a large pan. Add a knob of butter and cook the spinach for 2–3 minutes until the leaves are just wilted. Season. Drain off the excess liquid and arrange in the middle of warmed serving plates. Heat the remaining butter in a small pan until nutty-brown but not burnt and add a squeeze of lemon juice. Place two of the mackerel fillets on each serving of spinach and drizzle over the butter mixture, then spoon the chutney around the edge of the plates to serve.

63 Skate Fishcakes with Chilli Jam and Crème Fraîche

JAMES MARTIN'S FISH AND SHELLFISH RECIPE

Serves 4

350 g/12 oz potatoes, diced

1 large skate wing, filleted

200 ml/7 fl oz dry white wine

115 g/4 oz caster sugar

about 1 tsp sesame oil

3 tbsp dark soy sauce

1 tbsp clear honey

1 red chilli, seeded and finely chopped

1 tbsp white wine vinegar

25 g/1 oz unsalted butter

2 tbsp chopped fresh coriander

50 g/2 oz seasoned plain flour

2 eggs (preferably organic or free-range)

115 g/4 oz toasted fresh breadcrumbs

3 tbsp olive oil

2 limes

115 g/4 oz mixed fresh herb sprigs (such as dill, coriander, basil, chervil and flat-leaf parsley)

85 ml/3 fl oz double cream

salt and freshly ground black pepper

Crunchy fishcakes with a dollop of chilli jam and herb salad are one of the joys of eating. The fishcakes are made with skate-wing fillets – get your fishmonger to fillet them for you as it takes some strength. The chilli jam may lengthen the ingredient list but it's worth the effort.

1 Place the potatoes in a pan of boiling salted water, cover and simmer for 10–12 minutes until tender. Place the skate in a shallow pan, pour over the wine and then add just enough cold water to cover the fish. Bring to a gentle simmer and poach for 5–7 minutes until just tender but still moist.

2 Meanwhile, make the chilli jam. Place the caster sugar in a small pan and cook over a gentle heat until it caramelizes. Add a dash of the sesame oil, two tablespoons of the soy sauce, the honey, chilli and vinegar. Stir well to combine, then simmer gently for about 10 minutes until well reduced and thickened. If it becomes too dry, add a little boiling water and keep warm.

3 Remove the poached skate from the pan and set aside until cool enough to handle, then flake. When the potatoes are cooked, drain and then return to the pan for a couple of minutes to dry out. Mash until smooth, season to taste and beat in the butter and coriander. Fold in the flaked skate until well combined.

4 Shape the fish mixture into eight even-sized patties and toss in the seasoned flour. Beat the eggs in a shallow dish and add the patties, turning to coat, then coat them in the breadcrumbs. Arrange on a baking sheet and chill for at least 5 minutes (or up to 2 hours if time allows) to firm up.

5 Heat two tablespoons of the olive oil in a large frying pan and fry the fishcakes for 3 minutes on each side until heated through and golden brown. Meanwhile, prepare the garnish. Peel one of the limes and cut it into segments, then place in a bowl with the herb sprigs. Dress with the remaining dash of sesame oil and remaining tablespoon each of olive oil and soy sauce.

6 To make the crème fraîche, squeeze the juice from the remaining lime into a small bowl, whisk in the double cream and season to taste. Arrange the fishcakes on warmed serving plates with spoonfuls of the chilli jam and quenelles of the crème fraîche. Add a mound of the herb salad and serve.

64 Jerk Mullet with Pineapple Salsa

AINSLEY HARRIOTT'S FISH
AND SHELLFISH RECIPE

Serves 2

1 yellow pepper, halved,
seeded and chopped

2 red Scotch bonnet chillies,
seeded and finely chopped

1 garlic clove, roughly chopped

2.5 cm/1 in piece of fresh root
ginger, roughly chopped

$\frac{1}{2}$ tsp ground allspice

4 tbsp white wine vinegar

4 tbsp dark soy sauce

3 tbsp olive oil, plus a little extra

450 g/1 lb red mullet, cleaned,
scaled and fins removed

1 ripe baby pineapple

1 tbsp chopped fresh coriander

juice of 1 lime

salt and freshly ground black
pepper

Thai fragrant rice, to serve
(optional)

This dish is close to my heart because it is a real traditional Jamaican recipe, where my family is originally from. There the fish would be wrapped in banana leaves secured with cocktail sticks or foil to make a well-sealed parcel and barbecued over medium-hot coals for about 20 minutes, turning occasionally. Substitute red or grey snapper, salmon, trout or even sea bass for the mullet, if you wish.

1 Preheat the oven to 240°C/475°F/Gas 9 (fan oven 220°C from cold). To make the jerk seasoning, place the yellow pepper in a food processor with one of the chillies, the garlic and ginger and blitz until well blended. Add the allspice, vinegar, soy sauce and one tablespoon of the olive oil, then whizz again until smooth. Season to taste.

2 Cut several deep slashes into each side of the mullet and place in a lightly oiled shallow ovenproof dish. Pour over the jerk seasoning and rub it into the fish, making sure that some of it goes right down into the slashes. Bake for 12–15 minutes, or until the mullet is completely cooked through and tender.

3 Meanwhile, make the pineapple salsa. Peel the pineapple and remove the core, then cut the flesh into 1 cm/$\frac{1}{2}$ in cubes. Place in a bowl with the remaining chilli, two tablespoons of the oil, the coriander and lime juice. Season generously and mix well, then set aside at room temperature to allow the flavours to combine. For maximum effect serve the red mullet straight from the dish with separate bowls of pineapple salsa and Thai fragrant rice, if liked.

65 Hot Squid and Prawns with Coconut Gravy

LESLEY WATERS'S FISH AND
SHELLFISH RECIPE

Serves 4

675 g/1½ lb sweet potatoes, cut into thick, chunky chips

5 tbsp olive oil

4 tbsp dark soy sauce

pinch of freshly grated nutmeg (optional)

350 g/12 oz baby squid, cleaned

1 lime

1 tsp dried chilli flakes

225 g/8 oz raw peeled tiger prawns, veins removed, but with tails intact

2 tbsp madras curry paste

1 tbsp tomato purée

400 g/14 oz can coconut milk

175 g/6 oz baby spinach leaves

salt and freshly ground black pepper

This is one of my favourite ever *Ready Steady Cook* recipes. The flavours and textures are sensational and it is as delicious to eat as it is easy to prepare. It was a busy twenty minutes but with Ainsley's help I just about made it. I like to serve it with a pile of sweet potato chips.

1 Preheat the oven to 230°C/450°F/Gas 8 (fan oven 210°C from cold). Place the sweet potatoes in a pan of boiling salted water and par-boil for 4–5 minutes, then drain and tip into a large bowl. Add two tablespoons each of the olive oil and soy sauce, toss to combine and then transfer to a large roasting tin and season with black pepper and the nutmeg, if using. Bake for about 15 minutes until crisp and golden brown, turning occasionally to ensure they cook evenly.

2 To prepare the squid, cut off the tentacles and set aside. Cut each squid tube open and slash gently into the flesh in a lattice pattern using a small sharp knife and taking care not to cut too deeply.

3 Cut the lime in half and squeeze the juice from one half into a bowl, reserving the remainder to use in the gravy. Add the remaining three tablespoons of the olive oil and two tablespoons of the soy sauce with the chilli flakes and seasoning. Stir to combine, then add the prepared squid and prawns. Set aside for at least 5 minutes (or up to 30 minutes if time allows).

4 To make the gravy, heat a pan. Add the curry paste and tomato purée and fry for 30 seconds, stirring. Pour in the coconut milk and simmer for 5 minutes, stirring occasionally. Season to taste.

5 Meanwhile, heat a non-stick wok or large griddle pan. Add the squid and prawns with all their marinade and stir-fry over a high heat for 1–2 minutes until the squid is lightly seared and just tender. Continue to cook for another 1–2 minutes until the prawns have changed colour and are just cooked through.

6 Finish the gravy with a squeeze of lime juice and spoon into warmed large wide-rimmed bowls. Pile a small mound of spinach leaves into the centre of each and top with the spicy squid and prawns. Serve immediately with the sweet potato chips in a separate dish on the side.

66 Spaghetti in a Bag with Mussels

KEVIN WOODFORD'S FISH
AND SHELLFISH RECIPE

Serves 2

115 g/4 oz spaghetti (good quality)

about 3 tbsp olive oil

1 small onion, finely chopped

2 garlic cloves, crushed

½ tsp dried chilli flakes

¼ tsp fresh thyme leaves

85 ml/3 fl oz dry white wine

50 ml/2 fl oz fish stock

400 g/14 oz can chopped tomatoes (in rich tomato juice)

1 tbsp tomato purée

2 tbsp chopped mixed fresh herbs (such as basil, flat-leaf parsley and chives)

450 g/1 lb large fresh mussels, well cleaned

salt and freshly ground black pepper

I was given some truly superb authentic Italian pasta in this bag, and that's the trick to this simple dish: delicious pasta served with perfectly steamed mussels. Check the cooking instructions on the back of the spaghetti packet and cook it for about 4 minutes less than recommended. The sauce doesn't overpower the mussels, so their flavour can shine through.

1 Preheat the oven to 220°C/425°F/Gas 7 (fan oven 200°C from cold). Plunge the spaghetti into a large pan of boiling salted water and cook for about 8 minutes (see introduction) until almost but not quite tender.

2 Meanwhile, heat a sauté pan. Add two tablespoons of the oil, then tip in the onion and cook for 2–3 minutes until softened, stirring occasionally. Add the garlic, chilli flakes and thyme and cook for another minute, stirring. Pour in the wine and allow to bubble down, then add the stock, the tomatoes and tomato purée. Season to taste and bring to the boil, then reduce the heat and simmer for 5 minutes or until slightly reduced and thickened, stirring occasionally.

3 Cut out two 38 cm/15 in squares of non-stick baking paper and crumple them up into small balls, then open them out again. Drain the spaghetti and tip into the tomato sauce with the fresh herbs. Stir to mix, then spoon half on to each square of paper. Insert the mussels into the pasta and drizzle over the remaining olive oil.

4 Lift up opposite sides of the paper square and fold together, twisting and tucking the other ends to form a secure parcel. Place on a baking sheet and bake for 6–8 minutes until the bag has ballooned, all the mussels have opened (discard any that do not) and the spaghetti is completely tender. Arrange on warmed serving plates and serve immediately, allowing your guest to fold down the sides of the bag him or herself.

67 Turkey Saltimbocca with Herb Mash and Broad Beans

PAUL RANKIN'S POULTRY
AND GAME RECIPE

Serves 2

350 g/12 oz potatoes, roughly chopped

115 g/4 oz frozen broad beans

120 ml/4 fl oz extra virgin olive oil

2 tbsp roughly chopped fresh flat-leaf parsley, plus extra sprigs to garnish

3 tbsp torn fresh basil

2 tbsp balsamic vinegar

2 turkey fillets, about 225 g/ 8 oz in total

2 tbsp roughly chopped fresh sage

4 slices Parma ham

2 garlic cloves, finely chopped

salt and freshly ground black pepper

The contrast in this dish between the succulent turkey and the crispiness of the Parma ham is wonderful. Turkey is not only extremely cheap to buy but also very low in fat. However, it can be a bit lacking in the flavour department, which is why this recipe works so well. For a perfect match, I've served them with a garlic-infused, olive-oil mash and some marinated broad beans.

1 Place the potatoes in a pan of boiling salted water, cover and simmer for about 15 minutes or until tender. Cook the broad beans in a pan of boiling salted water for 1–2 minutes until tender. Drain well and cool under cold running water, then pop the beans out of their skins and place in a bowl.

2 Add two tablespoons of the olive oil to the broad beans with one tablespoon each of the parsley and basil and all the balsamic vinegar. Place in a small pan, season and set aside to marinate for 10–15 minutes, but no longer as the beans will lose their brilliant colour.

3 Heat a large frying pan over a medium heat. Cut each turkey fillet horizontally in half into two even-sized thin slices, then sprinkle over the sage and season with pepper and a little salt, remembering that Parma ham is quite salty. Wrap a slice of Parma ham around each slice of turkey and secure with a wooden cocktail stick. Add a thin film of oil to the pan and cook the wrapped turkey for 2–3 minutes on each side, until cooked through and lightly golden.

4 Meanwhile, finish making the mash. Gently simmer the remaining olive oil in a pan with the garlic for 5 minutes to infuse the flavours, but be careful not to allow the garlic to colour (or pop in the microwave on high for 2 minutes). Stir in the remaining parsley with the basil, then remove from the heat. When the potatoes are cooked, drain and return to their pan for a couple of minutes to dry out. Mash until smooth, then beat in the infused oil mixture and season to taste.

5 Reheat the broad beans to warm through. Pile the mash into the centre of two warmed serving plates and arrange the turkey saltimbocca on top. Spoon over the broad beans and garnish with parsley sprigs to serve.

68 Chicken Breasts with Bacon and Mushroom Stuffing

BRIAN TURNER'S POULTRY
AND GAME RECIPE

Serves 2

115 g/4 oz unsalted butter, diced and chilled

6 button mushrooms, very finely chopped

2 rindless streaky bacon rashers, finely chopped

2 boneless, skinless chicken breasts

2 tbsp seasoned plain flour

1 large egg

25 g/1 oz dried white breadcrumbs

1 tbsp olive oil

2 tbsp dry white wine

juice of ½ lemon

120 ml/4 fl oz double cream

2 tbsp chopped mixed fresh tarragon, chives and flat-leaf parsley

salt and freshly ground black pepper

steamed French beans and baby new potatoes, to serve

I like to prepare these stuffed chicken fillets well in advance and leave them to firm up and rest in the fridge before cooking them. They also look very attractive served fanned out on the plate on a classic potato galette. You can vary the stuffing depending on what ingredients you have to hand – don't be tempted to overfill them or they'll burst all over the pan. They are fantastic served with lemon butter sauce.

1 Preheat the oven to 200°C/400°F/Gas 6 (fan oven 180°C from cold). Heat a frying pan and melt half the butter. Add the mushrooms and bacon and cook for 3–4 minutes until lightly golden, stirring. Season and leave to cool a little.

2 Use a sharp knife to cut horizontally almost all the way through each chicken breast, leaving the fillet attached to one side. Stuff with the mushroom and bacon mixture. Seal and secure with a wooden cocktail stick. Place the seasoned flour on a plate, then place the egg in a shallow dish and lightly whisk it, and place the breadcrumbs in another shallow dish.

3 Heat a large ovenproof frying pan. Coat each stuffed chicken fillet in the seasoned flour, then dip in the beaten egg and finally coat in the breadcrumbs. Add the oil to the pan with a knob of the butter and cook the chicken for 3–4 minutes, turning once. Transfer to the oven and cook for another 6–8 minutes or until the chicken is cooked through and tender.

4 To make the lemon butter sauce, place the wine and lemon juice in a small pan and cook until reduced by half. Stir in the cream and simmer for another minute or so until slightly reduced, stirring. Add the remaining butter, a little at a time, whisking constantly until you have achieved a smooth sauce. Season to taste and stir in the herbs.

5 Carefully remove the cocktail sticks from each stuffed chicken breast and arrange on warmed serving plates with the green beans and baby new potatoes to the side. Spoon around the sauce and serve at once.

69 Chicken and Chickpea Tagine with Honey

JAMES MARTIN'S POULTRY
AND GAME RECIPE

Serves 2

4 large boneless, skinless chicken thighs or 2 boneless, skinless breasts

$1/2$ tsp each ground paprika, turmeric, cinnamon, ginger and cayenne pepper

1 tbsp clear honey

3 tbsp olive oil

1 small red onion, finely sliced

2 garlic cloves, finely chopped

2 ripe tomatoes, peeled, seeded and chopped

300 ml/$1/2$ pint chicken stock

400 g/14 oz can chickpeas, drained and rinsed

juice of $1/2$ lemon

2 tbsp chopped fresh coriander

1 tbsp chopped fresh mint

salt and freshly ground black pepper

steamed couscous, to serve (optional)

The combination of spicy chicken, tomatoes and chickpeas here is really successful, and the best thing about it is that it all gets cooked in one pot so there's little washing up. I've suggested serving it with steamed couscous, but bulgar wheat or, if you want to be really trendy, quinoa would be equally delicious. And don't just dress them with lemon. In Morocco, where the essence of their cooking is the exquisite combination of fruit and nuts, they use everything from sultanas to bananas and/or toasted nuts.

1 Trim down the chicken and cut into bite-sized pieces. Place in a bowl with the spices, honey and one tablespoon of the oil. Season generously, then stir well to combine and set aside for at least 5 minutes to allow the flavours to develop (or up to 24 hours covered with clingfilm in the fridge if time allows).

2 Heat the remaining two tablespoons of oil in a sauté pan with a lid, then sauté the onion and garlic for 4–5 minutes until softened and beginning to brown. Add the marinated chicken and sauté for a minute or two until just sealed and lightly browned.

3 Add half the tomatoes to the pan with the stock and chickpeas, then bring to the boil. Reduce the heat, cover and simmer for 8 minutes or until the chicken is completely tender and the sauce has slightly thickened, stirring occasionally. Season to taste.

4 Stir the remaining tomatoes into the pan and season to taste, then add the lemon juice, coriander and mint. Stir to combine and arrange on warmed serving plates with the couscous, if liked.

70 Pot-bellied Chicken

LESLEY WATERS'S POULTRY
AND GAME RECIPE

Serves 4

3 tbsp wholegrain mustard

1 tbsp clear honey

4 x 85 g/3 oz boneless, skinless chicken breasts

12 rindless smoked streaky bacon rashers

2 tbsp olive oil

200 ml/7 fl oz white wine

15 g/^{1}/$_2$ oz bunch of fresh tarragon, leaves roughly chopped

175 g/6 oz frozen petit pois

^{1}/$_2$ lemon, pips removed

200 ml/7 fl oz double cream

salt and freshly ground black pepper

This is a great one-pot dish. It's my take on the classic combination of chicken, bacon, tarragon and cream, which work extremely well together. You could prepare the wrapped chicken fillets up to 24 hours in advance, just ready to be cooked off. I like to serve this with mash, but roasted new potatoes or warm crusty bread with a bitter leaf salad also go very well with it.

1 Place the mustard in a small bowl with the honey and mix to form a paste. Spread each chicken breast all over with the mustard paste and then wrap in the streaky bacon rashers – you'll need three per fillet.

2 Heat the oil in a large non-stick frying pan or sauté pan with a lid. Add the wrapped chicken fillets and fry for 2–3 minutes on each side, until well browned all over. Pour in the white wine, add half of the tarragon, cover and cook for 5 minutes.

3 Remove the lid and scatter the petit pois over the pan, then add a squeeze of lemon juice. Pour over the cream and sprinkle the remaining tarragon on top. Season well and bring to the boil, then simmer for 5 minutes or until the chicken is completely tender and cooked through. Arrange the wrapped chicken fillets in warmed wide-rimmed serving bowls and spoon around some of the sauce to serve.

71 Bacon, Sage and Chicken Kebabs with Avocado Salsa

TONY TOBIN'S POULTRY AND GAME RECIPE

Serves 2

2 x 200 g/7 oz boneless, skinless chicken breasts, cut into 24 even-sized cubes

8 fresh sage leaves

4 rindless streaky bacon rashers, each cut into 3 pieces

about 1 tbsp olive oil

4 soft flour tortillas

shredded Little Gem lettuce and soured cream, to serve

FOR THE SALSA:

1 firm ripe avocado, peeled, stoned and finely diced

4 spring onions, finely chopped

2 tbsp chopped mixed fresh flat-leaf parsley and mint

2 tbsp olive oil

juice of 1 lime

pinch of chilli powder

salt and freshly ground black pepper

This is a fantastic combination of succulent chicken and bacon wrapped in soft flour tortillas with some crunchy lettuce, avocado salsa and a good dollop of soured cream. You'll need four 15 cm/6 in metal skewers, or bamboo skewers that have been soaked in water for at least 30 minutes, as the kebabs get finished in the oven. They would also work brilliantly on the barbecue.

1 Preheat the oven to 220°C/425°F/Gas 7 (fan oven 200°C from cold) and heat a griddle pan over a medium heat until smoking hot. Thread the chicken cubes on to four 15 cm/6 in metal or soaked bamboo skewers, alternating them with sage leaves and pieces of bacon.

2 Drizzle each skewer with a little oil, then place on the griddle pan and chargrill for 1–2 minutes on each side until nicely marked. Transfer to a small baking sheet and bake for 10–12 minutes or until the chicken is just tender and cooked through.

3 Meanwhile, make the salsa. Place all the ingredients in a bowl and stir gently to combine. Season to taste, cover with clingfilm and set aside at room temperature to allow the flavours to develop – just don't try to make this too far in advance or the avocado is in danger of going black.

4 Reheat the griddle pan. Add a soft flour tortilla and heat for 30 seconds, turning once, until soft and pliable. Repeat with the remaining tortillas and stack them up on a warmed plate. Arrange the chicken skewers on a warmed serving platter and hand around the avocado salsa, warmed tortillas, shredded lettuce and soured cream.

72 Aromatic Chicken Stir-fry

ANTONY WORRALL
THOMPSON'S POULTRY AND
GAME RECIPE

Serves 4

1 egg white

3 tbsp Chinese rice wine

4 tsp cornflour

4 tbsp sunflower oil

450 g/1 lb boneless, skinless chicken breasts, cut into 2.5 cm/1 in pieces

2 garlic cloves, finely chopped

2.5 cm/1 in piece of fresh root ginger, finely chopped

1/2 tsp dried chilli flakes

6 spring onions, sliced on the diagonal into 2.5 cm/1 in lengths

150 ml/1/4 pint chicken stock

2 tbsp dark soy sauce

pinch of sugar

225 g/8 oz Chinese vegetable medley, cut into 2.5 cm/1 in pieces

4 tbsp chopped mixed fresh coriander and basil

salt and freshly ground black pepper

oriental noodles, to serve (optional, see recipe page 59)

This bag was right up my street. It contained a packet of Chinese vegetable medley: pak choi, choi sum and tat soi. Numerous versions of Chinese mixed vegetables are now readily available, or you could use any selection of green vegetables, such as asparagus, sugarsnap peas, broccoli and Chinese cabbage, and blanch them briefly before use.

1 Place the egg white in a food processor with one tablespoon of the Chinese rice wine and a teaspoon of the cornflour. Blend for 1 minute, then pour over the chicken in a non-metallic dish. Cover with clingfilm and set aside for at least 10 minutes (up to 30 minutes in the fridge if time allows) – this is called velveting.

2 Place half the oil in a large pan with 1 litre/1 3/4 pints of water and bring to the boil. Drop in the chicken with a slotted spoon, stir and cook for 1 1/2 minutes. Drain on kitchen paper.

3 Heat a wok and swirl in the remaining oil. Add the garlic, ginger, chilli flakes and spring onions and stir-fry for 30 seconds, then add the drained chicken and stir-fry for 1 minute. Pour in the remaining rice wine with the stock, soy sauce and sugar and season generously.

4 Increase the heat and bring to the boil, then reduce to a simmer, add the vegetables and cook for 1–2 minutes until just tender but still crisp. Mix the remaining cornflour with one and a half tablespoons of water and stir into the wok. Cook for a minute or so until the sauce clears and thickens, then stir in the herbs. Ladle into warmed serving bowls and serve at once with the noodles, if liked.

73 Peking-style Duck with Pancakes

KEVIN WOODFORD'S
POULTRY AND GAME RECIPE

Serves 2

4 tbsp clear honey

juice of ½ lime

1 tbsp dark soy sauce

2 duckling breasts, skinned

85 g/3 oz plain flour

2 eggs (preferably organic or free-range)

about 3 tbsp sunflower oil

2 tsp sesame oil

1 small red onion, finely chopped

¼ tsp dried chilli flakes

50 g/2 oz light muscovado sugar

1 tbsp white wine vinegar

1 bunch of spring onions, cut into fine sticks

½ cucumber, seeded and cut into fine sticks

salt and freshly ground black pepper

This dish normally takes days to prepare, but under pressure on the show I came up with this version. It reflects the cosmopolitan influences in this country and will certainly impress guests.

1 To prepare the marinade, place the honey in a shallow non-metallic dish and add the lime juice and soy sauce, stirring to combine. Cut the duckling breasts in half horizontally then cut into strips and prick with a fork. Stir into the marinade, season with pepper and set aside for 5 minutes (or up to 24 hours if time allows).

2 To make the pancakes, place the flour in a bowl with a good pinch of salt. Make a well in the centre and gradually beat in the eggs with one tablespoon of the sunflower oil and about 50 ml/2 fl oz of cold water to make a smooth creamy batter. Allow to rest for 5 minutes (up to 2 hours in the fridge is perfect if possible).

3 Heat a non-stick wok over a medium heat until searing hot. Add the marinated duck, reserving the marinade, and stir-fry for 6–8 minutes until cooked through and caramelized, adding a few drops of water to the pan occasionally if the mixture starts to catch and burn. Remove from the heat and pile into a warmed serving dish. Set aside for a few minutes to allow the duck to rest.

4 Meanwhile, heat a heavy-based non-stick frying pan. Add a thin film of sunflower oil to the pan and then add a small ladleful of the pancake batter. Swirl around to form a pancake that is no more than 13 cm/5 in diameter. Cook for a minute or so until just set and lightly golden, then flip over and cook for another 30 seconds. Transfer to a warmed serving plate and continue until you have ten pancakes.

5 Heat the sesame oil in a small pan. Add the onion and chilli flakes, then cook for 2–3 minutes until softened, stirring. Sprinkle over the sugar, tossing to combine, and as the sugar begins to melt, stir in the vinegar and the reserved marinade. Cook gently for 3–4 minutes or until the sauce has thickened and become slightly sticky. Remove from the heat and pour into a serving bowl.

6 Serve the Peking duck with a stack of the pancakes, the bowl of caramelized red onion sauce and separate dishes of the spring onion and cucumber to serve. Let your guest take a pancake, smear on a small spoonful of sauce and top it with some of the vegetables and Peking duck before rolling it up to eat.

74 Tea-smoked Duck on Sweet Potato Mash

PHIL VICKERY'S POULTRY
AND GAME RECIPE

Serves 2

2 duck breasts, well trimmed (skin on)

50 g/2 oz light muscovado sugar, plus 2 tbsp

50 g/2 oz tea leaves

50 g/2 oz long-grain rice

450 g/1 lb sweet potatoes, chopped

150 ml/¼ pint red wine

2 tbsp olive oil

1 small red onion, cut into 6 wedges

115 g/4 oz purple sprouting broccoli

2 tsp dark soy sauce

50 g/2 oz unsalted butter, diced and chilled

salt and freshly ground black pepper

Tea-smoked duck has become rather trendy and now appears frequently on restaurant menus. Well, it's incredibly easy to make at home. If you want to prepare some of it in advance, simply smoke the duck for 8 minutes until almost but not quite tender, then finish off the cooking process in the oven or a heavy-based pan to serve.

1 Using a small sharp knife, lightly score the skin of each duck breast in a criss-cross pattern. Arrange them on a rack that will fit into a wok with a lid. Cut out two circles of foil about 20 cm/8 in in diameter. Place one on top of the other and scrunch up the sides so that you have a double-thickness container about 13 cm/5 in in diameter. Mix together the 50 g/2 oz of sugar with the tea and rice in a bowl, then pour into the foil container and place in the bottom of the wok.

2 Place the wok on the hob and turn up the heat to full and, once the tea starts smoking, add the rack with the duck. Cover with the lid and cook over a medium heat for 12 minutes or until the duck is cooked through and completely tender.

3 Meanwhile, cook the sweet potatoes in a covered pan of boiling salted water for 10–12 minutes until tender. Pour the wine into a small pan and bring to a simmer, then sprinkle in the remaining two tablespoons of sugar, stirring to melt. Continue to simmer for 4–5 minutes until reduced by two-thirds.

4 Heat the olive oil in a large frying pan, then add the onion, season and cook for about 5 minutes until softened and lightly caramelized, turning once. Cook the broccoli in a steamer for 3–4 minutes until just tender. Drain and keep warm.

5 Using tongs, remove the cooked duck from the wok and add to the pan with the onion, skin-side down. Cook for a minute or so until the skin is crispy and golden brown, then remove from the heat and leave to rest on a warm plate for a minute or two. Season to taste.

6 Drain the sweet potatoes then return them to the pan. Mash the potatoes with the soy sauce and spoon on to warmed serving plates. Whisk the butter into the reduced red wine and season to taste. Carve the duck into slices on the diagonal and fan out on the sweet potato mash. Add the onion wedges and steamed broccoli to the side and drizzle over the red wine sauce to serve.

75 Spatchcocked Poussin with Gremolata and Chips

ROSS BURDEN'S POULTRY
AND GAME RECIPE

Serves 2

sunflower oil, for deep-frying

2 poussins

450 g/1 lb potatoes

4 tbsp chopped fresh flat-leaf
parsley

2 garlic cloves, roughly chopped

grated rind of 1 orange

grated rind of 1 lemon

100 ml/3½ fl oz dry white wine

salt and freshly ground black
pepper

Poussins are very tender and quick to cook. Now you can buy them in most supermarkets already spatchcocked; or get your butcher to do it for you. Here I have started them in a griddle pan and finished roasting them in the oven to keep the flesh succulent and moist while the skin stays wonderfully crisp.

1 Preheat the oven to 220°C/425°F/Gas 7 (fan oven 200°C from cold) and a deep-fat fryer or a deep-sided pan one-third full of sunflower oil to 160°C/325°F. Heat two ovenproof griddle pans over a medium heat until searing hot.

2 Using poultry shears or sharp kitchen scissors, cut each poussin along the back and down each side of the backbone, then remove and discard the backbone. Snip the wishbone in half, then open out and snip out the ribs. Turn over, so it is skin-side up, and press down firmly on the breastbone with the heel of your hand to flatten out. Trim off any excess skin, rinse under the tap and dry well.

3 Season the spatchcocked poussins and then add to the heated griddle pans, skin-side down. Cook for 3 minutes, then using tongs turn the poussins over and transfer the pans to the oven. Roast the poussins for another 10 minutes or until cooked through with crisp, golden skin.

4 Meanwhile, cut the potatoes into chunky chips and rinse under the cold tap – this helps to remove the starch. Drain and dry thoroughly in a clean tea towel. Place the potatoes in a wire basket and carefully lower into the heated oil. Cook for 4 minutes only, until cooked through but not coloured. Drain well on kitchen paper.

5 Increase the temperature of the oil to 190°C/375°F. Meanwhile, make the gremolata. Mix the parsley, garlic, orange and lemon rind in a small bowl and season. Carefully transfer the griddle pans with the poussins back to the hob. Deglaze the pans with the wine, then sprinkle the gremolata over the poussins and leave to rest.

6 Tip the blanched chips back into the wire basket and carefully lower into the heated oil. Cook for a minute or two until crisp and golden brown. Drain well on kitchen paper and season with salt. Put the gremolata poussins on warmed serving plates, spoon around some of the reduced wine and pan juices, arrange the chips to the side and serve immediately.

76 Roast Goose with Seasonal Vegetables

AINSLEY HARRIOTT'S
POULTRY AND GAME RECIPE

Serves 2

1 goose breast, trimmed
(skin on)

2 x 225 g/8 oz potatoes

1 large parsnip, diced

175 ml/6 fl oz red wine

120 ml/4 fl oz chicken stock

grated rind of 1 orange

pinch of ground mixed spice

50 g/2 oz chilled unsalted
butter, diced

8 large Brussels sprouts,
trimmed and grated

1 garlic clove, crushed

120 ml/4 fl oz double cream

1 tbsp fresh thyme leaves

salt and freshly ground black
pepper

I devised this dish for Barbara Windsor when she came on the show for a festive celebrity special. Babs arrived in a fetching Santa costume and brought along traditional Christmas ingredients, expecting me to produce miracles in twenty minutes … This recipe was the result of my efforts, and worked out quite well if I say so myself. I called it 'Goosie Gander Windsor'.

1 Preheat the oven to 200°C/400°F/Gas 6 (fan oven 180°C from cold). Heat an ovenproof frying pan. Score the skin of the goose breast with a sharp knife and then add to the pan, skin-side down. Cook for a few minutes until lightly golden, then turn over and cook on the other side for 1–2 minutes until well sealed. Transfer to a wire rack. Set this on top of the frying pan so the fat can drain off and then bake for 10–15 minutes or until the goose is tender and cooked through.

2 Cut each potato into eight wedges and place in a pan of boiling salted water. Cover and cook for 6–8 minutes until just tender. Place the parsnip in a separate pan of boiling salted water and cook for 10–12 minutes until tender. Place the wine in another pan with the chicken stock, orange rind and mixed spice and boil fast until reduced by half. Heat half the butter in a small wok and add the Brussels sprouts and garlic. Stir-fry for 2–3 minutes until just tender, then stir in half of the cream and warm through. Season to taste.

3 Heat a large frying pan and drain the potatoes. Remove the goose from the oven and drain the excess fat into the pan. Leave the goose breast in a warm place to rest for at least 5 minutes. Add the thyme to the frying pan, then add the potato wedges and cook for 3–4 minutes on each side until lightly golden. Season to taste.

4 Drain the parsnips and place in a food processor with the remaining cream. Whizz until blended and season to taste. Carve the goose breast into slices and divide between warmed serving plates. Add dollops of the parsnip purée with the creamed stir-fried Brussels sprouts and potato wedges. Whisk the remaining butter into the reduced wine mixture to warm through, then drizzle the sauce around the plates to serve.

77 Venison Medallions with Chive Crushed Potatoes

AINSLEY HARRIOTT'S
POULTRY and GAME RECIPE

Serves 2

2 x 115 g/4 oz venison medallions

2 garlic cloves, cut into 10 slivers

10 tiny fresh rosemary sprigs

finely grated rind of 1 lemon

85 ml/3 fl oz olive oil

1 large leek, sliced on the diagonal

225 g/8 oz new potatoes, scrubbed

2 tbsp snipped fresh chives

salt and freshly ground black pepper

For maximum flavour marinate the venison, covered with clingfilm, in the fridge for up to 24 hours. The chive crushed potatoes make a wonderful accompaniment – it is a kind of textured mash so don't be tempted to make it too smooth. If you want to be really posh, spoon the potatoes into a 10 cm/4 in cooking ring set on the serving plates, but I have to say I don't usually bother.

1 Preheat the oven to 220°C/425°F/Gas 7 (fan oven 200°C from cold). Make five small incisions around the sides of each venison medallion. Insert the garlic slivers and rosemary sprigs. Season with pepper and sprinkle over half of the lemon rind, then drizzle over a tablespoon of the olive oil. Turn to coat the medallions evenly, then set aside to allow the flavours to combine.

2 Heat two tablespoons of the oil in an ovenproof frying pan. Add the leek and sauté for 3–4 minutes, then push them to one side and add the marinated venison medallions and quickly brown all over. Spread the leeks back over the bottom of the pan and sit the venison medallions on top, then transfer to the oven and roast for 5–10 minutes, depending on how rare you like your meat. Remove from the oven and leave to rest in a warm place.

3 Meanwhile, place the potatoes in a pan of boiling salted water and cook for 10–12 minutes until tender, then drain and place in a bowl. Add the remaining olive oil and, with the back of a fork, gently crush each potato until it just splits. Add the remaining lemon rind, season and then mix carefully until all the oil has been absorbed. Stir in the chives, and place a dollop of the potatoes in the centre of each warmed serving plate. Add a small mound of leeks on top and finish with a venison medallion. Serve at once.

78 Toad-in-the-Hole with Venison Sausages and Red Shallot Gravy

NICK NAIRN'S POULTRY
AND GAME RECIPE

Serves 2

2 venison sausages

4 tbsp sunflower oil

4 eggs (preferably organic or free-range)

150 ml/¼ pint milk

300 g/10 oz plain flour

1 banana shallot, finely chopped

120 ml/4 fl oz red wine

150 ml/¼ pint beef stock

1 tsp tomato purée

25 g/1 oz chilled unsalted butter, diced

salt and freshly ground black pepper

The secret of a good toad-in-the-hole is, of course, the batter: mixing it quickly and using it immediately. It is also crucial to heat the oil in the tin until it is smoking hot before pouring in the batter. A wide range of premium-quality sausages is now available in all major supermarkets. I think the venison ones are excellent, and might encourage people to try this undervalued game.

1 Preheat the oven to 220°C/425°F/Gas 7 (fan oven 200°C from cold) and heat a four-hole non-stick Yorkshire pudding tin. Twist each sausage in half and cut it to make four small sausages in total. Heat a little of the oil in a frying pan and brown the sausages all over for 2–3 minutes. Remove the tin from the oven and carefully pour a little of the oil into each hole. Return to the oven until the oil is smoking hot.

2 Meanwhile, whisk together the eggs and milk in a jug with 150 ml/¼ pint of water and season generously. Place the flour in a bowl and make a well in the centre. Pour the egg mixture into the well and gradually whisk in the flour. Quickly remove the tin from the oven and pour in the batter – just be careful because it's very hot. Top each one with a sausage and bake for about 15 minutes until the batter is well risen and golden brown.

3 To make the gravy, heat the remaining oil (about a tablespoon) in a small pan and sweat the shallot for 3–4 minutes until translucent and tender. Add the red wine and simmer for 2–3 minutes to reduce, then add the stock and tomato purée and continue to simmer for 5–6 minutes or until the gravy has slightly reduced and thickened. Just before serving, season to taste and whisk in the butter. Remove the toads-in-the-hole from the tin and arrange on warmed serving plates. Spoon over some of the gravy and serve at once.

79 Fillet Steak with Whisky Sauce and Pan-fried Potatoes

NICK NAIRN'S MEAT RECIPE

Serves 2

4 tbsp olive oil

250 g/9 oz baby new potatoes, quartered

2 garlic cloves, chopped

1 onion, thinly sliced

25 g/1 oz unsalted butter

2 fillet steaks, about 2.5 cm/ 1 in thick

2 tbsp Dijon mustard

1 tbsp cracked black peppercorns

2 tbsp whisky

85 ml/3 fl oz beef stock

50 ml/2 fl oz double cream

1 tbsp snipped fresh chives

2 tbsp shredded fresh basil

salt and freshly ground black pepper

steamed mangetout, to serve (optional)

This is a simple dish but a real masterpiece. When *One Foot in the Grave* star Richard Wilson came on the show we got on famously. He wanted to learn how to make classic pepper steak so that's what I did. The steak is carefully fried and then coated in buttery, creamy juices. Just that. Heaven! The secret is to crush the peppercorns coarsely in a coffee grinder and then tip into a fine sieve and shake out all the powder. This is important because otherwise the powder makes the steaks far too spicy.

1 Heat three tablespoons of the oil in a wok and sauté the potatoes and garlic for 5 minutes. Add the onion and continue to cook for another 5–10 minutes until the potatoes are cooked through and golden brown, tossing occasionally. Season well and keep hot.

2 Heat the remaining oil and the butter in a frying pan. Spread each steak with the Dijon mustard and roll in the cracked pepper to coat. Cook for 2–3 minutes each side, then add the whisky and ignite to flambé.

3 Transfer the steaks to a warm plate and leave to rest. Pour the stock into the pan and simmer for 4–5 minutes to thicken slightly. Reduce the heat, add the cream and chives and allow to bubble down and warm through. Season to taste.

4 Arrange each rested steak on a warmed serving plate and spoon over the whisky sauce. Stir the basil into the pan-fried potatoes and spoon on to the plate with some mangetout, if liked. Serve at once.

80 Chilli Beef Salad with Shoestring Potatoes

PAUL RANKIN'S MEAT RECIPE

Serves 2

sunflower oil, for deep-frying, plus 4 tbsp

3 tsp sesame oil

3 tbsp dark soy sauce

2 tsp clear honey

1 sirloin steak, about 4 cm/ 1½ in thick (about 300 g/ 10 oz in total)

1 large potato

115 g/4 oz button chestnut mushrooms

1 red chilli, seeded and thinly sliced

juice of 1 large lime (about 3 tbsp in total)

1 tsp caster sugar

few drops Tabasco

50 g/2 oz baby salad leaves

1 handful each of fresh chervil, flat-leaf parsley and dill fronds

salt and freshly ground black pepper

This colourful salad is bursting with flavours and interesting textures. Try to use organic or grass-fed beef that has been properly hung. For the potatoes you need a mandolin cutter or a food processor with the correct attachment because it is difficult to get them right by hand. Mandolins have come down in price recently and you should be able to pick one up inexpensively – just be careful of your fingers.

1 Preheat a deep-fat fryer or a deep-sided pan one-third full of sunflower oil to 160°C/320°F. Place two teaspoons of the sesame oil in a shallow dish with two teaspoons of the soy sauce and the honey and season with pepper. Whisk to combine and add the steak, turning to coat. Set aside for at least 5 minutes to allow the flavours to penetrate (or up to 24 hours if time allows).

2 Preheat a griddle pan over a medium-high heat until it is smoking hot. Remove the steak from the sesame mixture, shaking off any excess, and add to the pan. Chargrill for 2–3 minutes on each side, a little longer if you prefer your steak more well done. Transfer to a plate and season with salt.

3 Peel the potato and then using a mandolin or a food processor with an attachment blade, cut it into long, thin strips so they resemble shoestrings (fine julienne). Deep-fry the potato shoestrings for 3–4 minutes until golden brown. Meanwhile, heat a frying pan. Drain the potato on plenty of kitchen paper and season to taste. Add a tablespoon of the sunflower oil to the heated frying pan, then add the mushrooms and chilli. Season and sauté for 2–3 minutes, adding a tablespoon of the lime juice and a teaspoon of the soy sauce and tossing to coat.

4 To prepare the dressing, place the remaining two tablespoons of lime juice in a small bowl with the sugar and whisk until dissolved. Add the remaining two tablespoons of soy sauce, teaspoon of sesame oil and three tablespoons of sunflower oil with the Tabasco, then season with pepper and whisk until emulsified.

5 Place the salad leaves in a serving bowl with the herbs and coat with the salad dressing. Season generously and toss until lightly dressed. Spoon over the mushroom and chilli mixture and scatter the shoestring potatoes on top. Slice the rested steak on the diagonal, cutting away and discarding any fat, then scatter on top. Serve immediately.

81 Hot Pork Balls with Red Pepper Sauce

LESLEY WATERS'S MEAT
RECIPE

Serves 4

1 large red pepper, quartered and seeded

500 g/1 lb 2 oz lean minced pork

50 g/2 oz fresh white breadcrumbs

2 teaspoons ground coriander

1–2 tsp dried chilli flakes

1 egg, beaten

3 tbsp olive oil

1 large red onion, thickly sliced

1 garlic clove, crushed

1½ tsp paprika

1 tbsp tomato ketchup

1 tbsp tomato purée

300 ml/½ pint red wine

about 300 ml/½ pint vegetable stock

salt and freshly ground black pepper

plain boiled rice or noodles, to serve

soured cream and fresh coriander leaves, to garnish

A little goes a long way with this richly flavoured dish, especially when you add all the trimmings. Minced pork is underrated and I can't understand why. It's lean and healthy with bags of flavour. Use as many or as few dried chilli flakes as you want, depending on how hot you like your food – they do pack a powerful punch.

1 Preheat the oven to 200°C/400°F/Gas 6 (fan oven 180°C from cold). Finely chop a quarter of the pepper and then slice the remainder. Set the sliced pepper to one side and place the chopped pepper, minced pork, breadcrumbs, ground coriander, chilli flakes and egg in a food processor. Season generously and whizz together until blended. Using wet hands, divide the mixture into sixteen even-sized portions and then roll into balls.

2 Heat two tablespoons of the oil in a large, non-stick ovenproof frying pan and fry the pork balls for 3–4 minutes until sealed and lightly browned. Transfer the pan to the oven and bake for a further 10–12 minutes or until the pork balls are completely tender and cooked through.

3 Meanwhile, heat the remaining tablespoon of the oil in a large non-stick frying pan. Add the reserved pepper slices with the onion and cook for 4–5 minutes until softened, stirring occasionally. Add the garlic and paprika and cook for 30 seconds, stirring, then stir in the ketchup, tomato purée, red wine and half the stock. Season and bring to the boil, then cook over a high heat for 5–10 minutes or until well reduced to form a shiny, chunky sauce, adding a little more stock if necessary. Season to taste.

4 Spoon some rice or noodles on to warmed serving plates and top each serving with four of the pork balls. Spoon over the sauce and garnish with a drizzle of soured cream and some fresh coriander leaves. Serve immediately.

82 Smoky Sausage Cassoulet

KEVIN WOODFORD'S
MEAT RECIPE

Serves 4

3 tbsp olive oil

1 large onion, finely chopped

115 g/4 oz piece smoky bacon, diced

6 large ripe tomatoes, roughly chopped, or 400 g/14 oz can chopped tomatoes (or a mixture of both)

1 tbsp tomato purée

1 tbsp wholegrain mustard

400 g/14 oz can butter beans, drained and rinsed

8 butcher's-style spicy pork sausages (good quality)

2 thick slices rustic bread, crusts removed (about 85 g/ 3 oz in total)

handful of mixed fresh herbs (such as basil, flat-leaf parsley and chives)

25 g/1 oz unsalted butter

50 g/2 oz Gruyère, finely grated

salt and freshly ground black pepper

This is a variation on one of my all-time childhood favourites, sausages and onion gravy, but the addition of a stronger-flavoured sausage and the tangy tomato sauce makes it a treat for adults too. It is now easier to buy high-quality sausages than it has been for years. There has been something of a renaissance in them, and quite rightly so, with butchers and supermarkets expanding into herb, garlic and spicy varieties – good news for us all.

1 Preheat the grill to hot. Heat two tablespoons of the oil in a large pan. Add the onion and bacon and cook for about 5 minutes or until the onion has softened and the bacon is cooked through and lightly golden, stirring occasionally.

2 Add the tomatoes to the pan with the tomato purée and mustard, then season, stirring to combine. Bring to a simmer and cook for about 5 minutes or until all the flavours are well combined, stirring occasionally. Stir in the butter beans and cook for another couple of minutes until heated through.

3 Meanwhile, heat the remaining tablespoon of oil in a separate frying pan and cook the sausages for 6–8 minutes until tender and golden brown, turning occasionally.

4 Blitz the bread in a food processor with the herbs. Tip into a bowl. Melt the butter in a small pan and stir it into the crumbs, then stir in the Gruyère to combine. Add the sausages to the tomato and bean mixture, spoon into an oven-proof dish and scatter the breadcrumb mixture on top. Place under the grill until bubbling and golden brown. Serve at once.

83 Spiced Pork Steaks on Champ Patties with Sweet Pear Salsa

PHIL VICKERY'S MEAT RECIPE

Serves 2

2 potatoes, diced

2 tbsp light muscovado sugar

1 tsp coriander seeds

4 whole cloves

1 tsp allspice berries

115 g/4 oz ready-to-eat dried pears

2 x 175 g/6 oz pork steaks (preferably organic or free-range)

1 tsp paprika

pinch of ground cumin

50 g/2 oz unsalted butter, diced

sunflower oil, for frying

4 spring onions, finely sliced

150 ml/¼ pint double cream

1 egg yolk

1 tbsp chopped fresh flat-leaf parsley

4 tbsp seasoned flour

1 tsp wholegrain mustard

2 tbsp snipped fresh chives

salt and freshly ground white pepper

I called this one 'Pork from Cork' on the show in honour of the Irish contestant, Fergal O'Mullane. He had brought in all his favourite ingredients, hoping that I would be inspired. Luckily, I love this kind of food, full of gutsy, strong flavours, but it's not for anyone who is on a diet, especially when served with the mustard and chive cream.

1 Preheat the oven to 220°C/425°F/Gas 7 (fan oven 200°C from cold). Cook the potatoes for 10–12 minutes in a covered pan of boiling salted water until tender. Place the sugar in a small pan with 150 ml/¼ pint of water and the coriander seeds, cloves and allspice berries. Bring to a simmer, stirring until the sugar has melted, then stir in the pears, reduce the heat and simmer gently for 10–15 minutes or until the pears are completely tender and softened.

2 Heat a large ovenproof frying pan until hot. Flatten the pork steaks using a meat mallet or rolling pin covered in clingfilm. Place the paprika in a small bowl with the cumin and season generously, then tip on to a plate and use to coat the pork steaks. Add a knob of the butter and a little oil to the heated pan and sauté the pork for a minute or two on each side until well seared. Transfer to the oven and roast for another 4–6 minutes until cooked through and completely tender. Remove from the oven and leave to rest for a couple of minutes.

3 Melt a knob of the butter in a large non-stick frying pan and sauté the spring onions for one minute until softened. Add two tablespoons of the cream and simmer until reduced by half. Drain the potatoes and return to their pan for a couple of seconds to dry out, then mash. Stir in the spring onion mixture with the egg yolk and parsley, then season. Wipe out the frying pan and return to the heat. Using lightly floured hands, mould the potato mixture into two patties and dust with the seasoned flour. Melt a knob of the butter in the heated frying pan with a little oil and cook the patties for 2–3 minutes on each side until golden brown.

4 Drain the pears, discarding the syrup, and set aside to cool a little, then finely dice. Place the remaining cream in a small pan and whisk in the mustard and season to taste. Simmer to reduce by one-third, then whisk in the remaining butter and the chives and season to taste. Place a potato cake on each warmed serving plate and place a pork steak on top. Scatter around the sweet pear salsa and then spoon around the mustard and chive cream to serve.

84 Pork Chops with Marmalade Cream

ROSS BURDEN'S MEAT RECIPE

Serves 2

1 tbsp olive oil

2 x 150 g/5 oz pork loin chops, about 2.5 cm/1 in thick (organic or free-range, if possible)

50 ml/2 fl oz white wine or Cognac

2 carrots, thinly sliced

25 g/1 oz unsalted butter

1 tsp caster sugar

1 tbsp marmalade (good quality)

120 ml/4 fl oz double cream

salt and freshly ground black pepper

steamed baby new potatoes, to serve (optional)

My local butcher sells only traditionally reared free-range pork, but not everyone is as lucky as me. Thankfully the supermarkets finally seem to be listening and most now offer good ranges of decently reared pork. It may be at a premium price but is worth every extra penny in my book. The flavour combination here is not as strange as it sounds – if you think about it, marmalade is nothing more than caramelized bitter oranges. The resulting flavour is surprisingly subtle and works beautifully with the well-flavoured pork.

1 Heat the oil in a heavy-based frying pan. Trim away the skin and bone from the pork chops, then score the remaining fat with a sharp knife. Cook the pork chops for 4–5 minutes on each side or until tender and cooked through. Add the wine or Cognac, quickly ignite and flambé. Transfer the pork to a warm plate and allow to rest in a warm place, draining any juices back into the pan.

2 Meanwhile, place the carrots in a pan and cover with boiling salted water. Add the butter and sugar and return to the boil. Reduce to a simmer and cook for 3–4 minutes until just tender. Drain and season to taste.

3 Stir the marmalade into the flambéed mixture, scraping the pan with a wooden spoon to dislodge any sediment. Stir in the cream, season generously and allow to bubble down for 1 minute. Return the pork to the pan and baste for a few minutes to allow all the flavours to combine. Transfer the pork chops to warmed serving plates and spoon over the marmalade sauce. Add the carrots to the side and new potatoes, if liked. Serve at once.

85 Seared Calf's Liver with Balsamic Vinegar and Onions

JAMES MARTIN'S MEAT
RECIPE

Serves 2

2 tbsp olive oil

50 g/2 oz unsalted butter

**1 large Spanish onion, thinly
sliced**

300 ml/½ pint red wine

300 ml/1½ pint beef stock

**2 x 175 g/6 oz calf's liver
slices, each about 1 cm/½ in
thick**

4 tbsp balsamic vinegar

**salt and freshly ground black
pepper**

**Dijon-flavoured mash, to serve
(optional)**

I love calf's liver but on *Ready Steady Cook* it is nearly impossible to win with it. This recipe was the exception. The most important thing to remember when cooking liver is to do it quickly, which creates all those wonderful, sweet flavours. Chefs call it caramelizing; my mum calls it burnt. I think this is perfect served with lots of creamy mash flavoured to taste with Dijon mustard, but Ainsley's potato and bacon röstis (see recipe page 42) would be equally good.

1 Heat one tablespoon of the oil and half the butter in a sauté pan. Add the onion and sauté over a fairly high heat for 1–2 minutes until just beginning to soften. Pour in the red wine and allow it to bubble down for one minute, stirring, then add the stock and continue to simmer until the liquid has reduced by four-fifths, stirring occasionally.

2 When the onions are nearly ready, heat a frying pan over a medium heat until very hot. Add the remaining oil and a knob of the butter, then quickly cook the calf's liver until golden brown but still pink in the middle, turning once – this should take no more than 2 minutes, but if you prefer it well done cook for slightly longer. Leave to rest in the pan for a minute or two, then season to taste.

3 Pour the balsamic vinegar into the onion mixture and season to taste, then stir in the remaining knob of butter. Arrange the liver on serving plates with the Dijon mash, if liked. Spoon over the onion gravy and serve at once.

86 Spicy Lamb and Feta Salad with Sweet and Sour Dressing

TONY TOBIN'S MEAT RECIPE

Serves 2

$\frac{1}{2}$ **tsp each coriander seeds and dried chilli flakes**

1 tsp ground turmeric

$\frac{1}{4}$ **tsp ground cayenne, paprika and ginger**

2 garlic cloves, finely chopped

finely grated rind of 1 orange

1 tbsp clear honey

2 x 150 g/5 oz lamb leg steaks

about 5 tbsp olive oil

2 tsp light muscovado sugar

1 baby red pepper, seeded and diced

1 tbsp balsamic vinegar

4 fresh basil leaves, shredded

200 g/7 oz feta cheese, cut into cubes

2 tsp fresh lime juice

150 g/5 oz baby spinach leaves

4 spring onions, thinly sliced

salt and freshly ground black pepper

This dish is full of clean, refreshing flavours and, despite the fairly long list of ingredients, is incredibly easy to prepare. It is perfect for a balmy summer's evening, served warm or at room temperature with chunks of rustic bread to mop up the delicious juices.

1 Place the coriander seeds and chilli flakes in a mortar and crush with the pestle. Tip into a shallow dish and stir in the remaining spices, garlic, orange rind and honey. Use to coat the lamb steaks and then bash each one into an escalope using a meat mallet or rolling pin wrapped in clingfilm. Cut the escalopes into strips, discarding any excess fat.

2 Heat a wok or sauté pan over a medium heat until searing hot. Add one tablespoon of the oil and use to coat the bottom of the pan in a thin film, then tip in the lamb strips. Stir-fry for 5–6 minutes or until tender and caramelized.

3 Meanwhile, make the dressing. Place the sugar in a small pan and gently melt over a low heat. Stir in the diced pepper and leave to caramelize, tossing occasionally. Pour in three tablespoons of the oil and the balsamic vinegar, swirling the pan to combine. Remove from the heat and stir in the basil.

4 Place the feta in a large bowl. Drizzle over the remaining tablespoon of oil and add the lime juice. Season generously, and gently fold in the spinach and spring onions, then the lamb strips. Arrange on warmed serving plates, drizzle around the dressing and serve at once.

87 Mini Lamb Pies

BRIAN TURNER'S
MEAT RECIPE

Serves 4

1 tbsp olive oil, plus extra for brushing

1 onion, finely chopped

450 g/1 lb lean minced lamb

1 heaped tbsp tomato ketchup

1 tsp Worcestershire sauce

3 egg yolks

1 large potato, scrubbed (about 225 g/8 oz)

knob of unsalted butter

1 tbsp plain flour

120 ml/4 fl oz double cream

1 tsp Dijon mustard

50 g/2 oz Cheddar, finely grated

salt and freshly ground black pepper

buttered peas, to serve

Not unlike a shepherd's pie but with a topping more likely to be associated with moussaka, this robustly flavoured dish is the perfect comfort food for the colder months of the year, and the brilliant thing about it is that it takes only twenty minutes from start to finish. Each 'pie' is layered up in a metal cooking ring, which I think makes a homely dish like this good enough to grace a dinner-party table.

1 Preheat the oven to 240°C/475°F/Gas 9 (fan oven 220°C from cold) and preheat the grill to medium. Heat a frying pan and add the oil, then cook the onion for 2–3 minutes until softened but not coloured, stirring occasionally. Leave to cool a little. Put the lamb in a bowl and tip in the onion, ketchup, Worcestershire sauce and one of the egg yolks, then, using your hands, mix until well combined. Season. Place four 10 cm/4 in lightly oiled cooking rings on a baking sheet and divide the lamb mixture among them, pressing down with the back of a spoon. Place in the oven and bake for 10 minutes or until tender and cooked through.

2 Meanwhile, thinly slice the potato and place in a pan of boiling salted water. Cover and simmer for 6–8 minutes or until just tender. Heat the butter in a small pan, stir in the flour and cook for a minute, continuing to stir, then gradually pour in the cream a little at a time, stirring until smooth after each addition. Beat in the remaining two egg yolks with the Dijon mustard and Cheddar. Season to taste.

3 Remove the lamb from the oven. Drain the potatoes and arrange them in an overlapping layer on top of the lamb, then spoon over some of the Cheddar sauce and place under the grill for a minute or two until bubbling and lightly golden. Using a fish slice, transfer the pies on to warmed serving plates and carefully remove the cooking rings. Arrange some of the peas on the side to serve.

88 Fragrant Lamb with Herbed Couscous

ANTONY WORRALL
THOMPSON'S MEAT RECIPE

Serves 2

225 g/8 oz lamb fillet

1 tsp each ground ginger and paprika

1½ tsp ground turmeric

3 tbsp olive oil

1 small onion, finely chopped

2 garlic cloves, finely sliced

200 g/7 oz chestnut mushrooms, sliced

½ tsp each dried chilli flakes and ground cumin

100 ml/3½ fl oz chicken stock

FOR THE COUSCOUS:

200 g/7 oz couscous

3 tbsp extra virgin olive oil

juice of 1 lemon

300 ml/½ pint chicken stock

pinch of saffron stamens

2 tbsp chopped fresh flat-leaf parsley and chives

salt and freshly ground black pepper

thick Greek yoghurt and fresh coriander leaves, to garnish

To celebrate the 1,000th edition of *Ready Steady Cook* we ran a competition in *BBC Good Food Magazine* and the lucky winner, Mel Owen Turner, got to come on the show as a contestant. Luckily she was a big fan and brought me a very nice selection of ingredients, which just screamed Moroccan. Obviously it isn't possible to prepare a tagine in 20 minutes but I did manage a rather special 'cheat's' version using a lovely piece of lamb fillet.

1 Preheat the oven to 200°C/400°F/Gas 6 (fan oven 180°C from cold). Trim the excess fat from the lamb. Mix together the ginger and paprika and one teaspoon of the turmeric, then rub this into the lamb, adding a little salt. Heat one tablespoon of the oil in an ovenproof frying pan and brown the lamb on all sides. Transfer to the oven and cook for 8 minutes until just tender. Remove and leave to rest for a couple of minutes.

2 Meanwhile, heat a frying pan and add the remaining two tablespoons of oil. Sauté the onion, garlic and mushrooms for 5 minutes until tender, stirring. Season with salt, then stir in the remaining turmeric with the chilli flakes and cumin and cook for another few minutes, continuing to stir.

3 To make the couscous, place it in a large bowl and add half the extra virgin olive oil and the lemon juice. Mix well, ensuring that all the grains are completely coated. Heat the stock in a small pan with the saffron and season generously. Pour over the couscous and allow to sit in a warm place for 6–8 minutes until all the liquid has been absorbed, stirring occasionally.

4 Add the stock to the mushroom mixture and increase the heat slightly to reduce the sauce. Slice the lamb and stir it in until just warmed through – do not allow the mixture to reboil or the lamb will toughen. Fluff up the couscous and stir in the remaining extra virgin olive oil and the herbs. Season to taste. Arrange on warmed serving plates with the lamb. Garnish with a dollop of the Greek yoghurt and coriander leaves to serve.

89 Korma Lamb Biryani

AINSLEY HARRIOTT'S
MEAT RECIPE

Serves 4

1 tsp ground turmeric

2 tsp medium-hot curry powder

2 tbsp sunflower oil

3 tbsp chopped fresh coriander

350 g/12 oz boneless lean lamb, cubed

25 g/1 oz unsalted butter

1 onion, finely chopped

50 g/2 oz cashew nuts

225 g/8 oz basmati rice

2 tbsp raisins

600 ml/1 pint hot lamb or chicken stock

25 g/1 oz creamed coconut, grated

115 g/4 oz frozen peas

salt and freshly ground black pepper

This is a southern variation on the classic lamb biryani, adding some coconut along with a handful of cashew nuts and raisins. I love to eat this with a 'chutney' of yoghurt flavoured with finely chopped spring onions, freshly grated root ginger, crushed garlic and a handful of fresh chopped mint and coriander, and a salad of chopped tomatoes and green chillies with lime wedges on the side. A table naan and you've got a feast fit for a king!

1 Place the turmeric in a bowl with the curry powder and one tablespoon each of the oil and fresh coriander. Add the lamb and toss to coat. Set aside to allow the flavours to combine for as long as time allows (up to 24 hours is fine, covered with clingfilm in the fridge).

2 Heat the remaining tablespoon of oil in a sauté pan with a tight-fitting lid, add the butter and, once it has stopped sizzling, tip in the onion. Cook for 4–5 minutes until softened and just beginning to brown at the edges. Add the lamb with the cashew nuts, then cook over a high heat for 2–3 minutes until the lamb is sealed and lightly browned.

3 Stir the rice and the raisins into the pan and cook for another 30 seconds or so, stirring. Pour in the stock and add the creamed coconut, then bring to the boil. Stir once, reduce the heat, cover tightly and simmer gently for 8–10 minutes until the rice is almost tender and most of the stock has been absorbed.

4 Gently fork the peas into the top of the rice mixture, cover again and cook for another 2–3 minutes or until all the stock has been absorbed and the lamb is completely tender. Fluff up the biryani with a fork and season to taste, then turn out on to a serving dish and scatter over the remaining coriander to serve.

90 Pavlova Nests with Peaches and Strawberries

AINSLEY HARRIOTT'S DESSERT

Serves 2

2 egg whites

pinch of cornflour

2 drops of white wine vinegar

115 g/4 oz icing sugar, sifted

225 ml/8 fl oz dry white wine

1 vanilla pod, split

1 tbsp clear honey

1 firm ripe peach, peeled and sliced

115 g/4 oz strawberries, hulled, halved if large

about 4 tsp thick Greek yoghurt

When prima ballerina Darcey Bussell came on the show with a wonderful selection of seasonal fruits, I just had to make her a version of this famous dessert. Legend goes that it was originally devised by an Australian chef called Herbert Sachse for the Russian ballerina Anna Pavlova. The built-up sides of the dessert are meant to resemble a tutu. Use any fruit you fancy, but I think this combination works well with the sweetness of the Pavlova.

1 Preheat the oven to 170°C/325°F/Gas 3 (fan oven 150°C from cold). Line a baking sheet with non-stick baking paper. Whisk the egg whites to stiff peaks. Whisk in the cornflour, vinegar and icing sugar, a spoonful at a time, until the mixture is thick and glossy. Spoon it into a piping bag fitted with a 2.5 cm/1 in fluted nozzle, and pipe two meringue nests, a little apart, on to the lined baking sheet. Bake for 15–20 minutes until firm.

2 Meanwhile, heat the wine in a pan with the vanilla pod and honey. Add the peach slices and poach for 1–2 minutes until just tender. Tip in the strawberries, stirring to combine, then remove from the heat and set aside to allow the flavours to mingle.

3 Place the meringue nests on serving plates and use a slotted spoon to fill with the poached fruits. Add a dollop of the yoghurt on top and drizzle around a little of the syrup to serve.

91 Italian Meringue Baked Alaska with Summer Berries

JAMES MARTIN'S DESSERT

Serves 4

225 g/8 oz caster sugar

50 g/2 oz unsalted butter

175 g/6 oz digestive biscuits

500 ml/18 fl oz tub vanilla ice cream, softened slightly at room temperature

225 g/8 oz raspberries

2 tbsp icing sugar, plus extra for dusting

4 egg whites

mixed summer berries and fresh mint sprigs, to decorate

Ainsley doesn't like it when I make Italian meringue as the food mixer ends up being on full whack for most of the programme. But for me this Baked Alaska is worth the effort and aggravation.

1 To make the Italian meringue, place the sugar with six tablespoons of water in a heavy-based pan and bring slowly to the boil, without stirring. If sugar crystals get stuck to the side of the pan, brush them down into the syrup with a pastry brush dipped in cold water. Now increase the temperature so that the syrup cooks rapidly. Insert the sugar thermometer, if one is available, to check the temperature with later.

2 Meanwhile, prepare the base. Melt the butter in a small pan, and crush the biscuits in a food processor or a polythene bag with a rolling pin. Stir the crushed biscuits into the melted butter, then spoon the crumbs into a pile in the centre of a large serving dish. Press the crumbs into a 15 cm/6 in disc that is at least 5 mm/¼ in thick. Place the softened ice cream on top of the base and carefully mould with a palette knife briefly dipped in boiling water – do not press too hard or the base will break. Place in the freezer until ready to use.

3 To make the raspberry coulis, tip most of the raspberries into a food processor (reserving a few to decorate) with two tablespoons of water and the icing sugar. Blend to a purée, then pass through a sieve into a serving jug. Set aside.

4 When the sugar syrup reaches 110°C/220°F, beat the egg whites in the bowl of a food mixer until stiff, and when the sugar syrup reaches 120°C/240°F, remove the pan from the heat. If you haven't got a sugar thermometer, drop a teaspoon of syrup into cold water. It is ready when it forms a firm but soft ball that can be squeezed between your fingers. Switch the food mixer back on to whisk, then pour the hot syrup on to the egg white in a steady stream. Continue to whisk until the mixture is stiff and shiny. When the whisk is lifted, the meringue should have no movement. Spoon into a large piping bag fitted with a 2.5 cm/1 in plain nozzle and pile around the ice cream until completely smothered.

5 Use a blowtorch to finish off the meringue and give it an even, golden colour. Decorate with the reserved raspberries, summer berries and mint sprigs. Add a light dusting of icing sugar and serve immediately, handing round the raspberry coulis separately.

92 Lemon Cake with Pineapple

LESLEY WATERS'S DESSERT

Serves 4–6

115 g/4 oz caster sugar, plus extra for dusting

115 g/4 oz unsalted butter, softened, plus extra for greasing

2 eggs (preferably organic or free-range), beaten

finely grated rind of 1 lemon

1 tsp ground ginger

115 g/4 oz self-raising flour

2–3 tbsp milk

1 ripe pineapple, peeled, cored and thickly sliced

1 tbsp clear honey

juice of ½ orange

100 ml/3½ fl oz double cream

150 g/5 oz thick Greek yoghurt

1–2 tablespoons icing sugar to taste, plus extra for dusting

This cake is best eaten just warm and not long out of the oven, which is just as well considering I had only twenty minutes from start to finish on the show. However, I was really pleased with the end result: a wonderfully indulgent dessert, perfect for a tea-time treat or as a dinner-party finale.

1 Preheat the oven to 200°C/400°F/Gas 6 (fan oven 180°C from cold). Grease two 20 cm/8 in non-stick sandwich tins and lightly dust with caster sugar, shaking out the excess. Set aside.

2 Place the butter in a food processor with the sugar and blitz to combine. Pour in the eggs through the feeder tube, then add the lemon rind and ginger. Tip in the flour and milk, then pulse briefly to combine. Divide between the prepared tins and bake for 12–14 minutes until well risen and golden brown.

3 Meanwhile, heat a griddle pan. Add the pineapple slices and cook for 4–5 minutes, turning halfway through cooking time. Remove the pan from the heat and allow to cool slightly. Mix together the honey and orange juice in a small bowl and pour over the pineapple in the warm pan, turning to coat.

4 To make the filling for the cake, place the cream in a bowl and lightly whip. Fold in the yoghurt and the icing sugar to taste.

5 When the cakes are baked, turn them out on to a wire rack and leave to cool a little, then spread the cream filling over each half. Top one half with half of the pineapple slices that have been tossed again in the orange syrup, and sandwich the two halves together. Arrange the rest of the pineapple slices on top, dust with icing sugar, then cut into slices and arrange on serving plates. Enjoy!

93 Vanilla-scented Pears with Raspberry Zabaglione

KEVIN WOODFORD'S
DESSERT

Serves 2

600 ml/1 pint dry white wine

225 g/8 oz caster sugar

1 vanilla pod

finely grated rind and juice of 1 lemon

2 ripe firm Comice pears

115 g/4 oz raspberries

1 tbsp icing sugar, plus extra for dusting

2 egg yolks

fresh mint sprigs, to decorate

A combination of pears and light zabaglione laced with a raspberry purée will revive even the most jaded palate. Put some zest in your life! It is crucial that the pears are covered completely with liquid while they are being poached. Add a little extra boiling water to the pan if necessary and fit a circle of non-stick baking paper over the pears to help prevent evaporation.

1 Place 500 ml/18 fl oz of the wine in a small deep-sided pan with 175 g/6 oz of the sugar, the vanilla pod and lemon rind and juice. Bring to the boil, then reduce the heat, stirring until the sugar has dissolved.

2 Meanwhile, peel the pears, leaving the stalks on, then remove the cores through the base, keeping the pears intact. Add the pears to the pan, cover with a round of non-stick baking paper and then a lid, and poach for about 10 minutes or until just tender, turning occasionally.

3 Place the remaining wine and sugar in a small pan and simmer gently for a few minutes until the sugar has dissolved, stirring. Increase the heat and cook until the wine mixture has reduced by one third.

4 Reserve some of the raspberries for decoration and place the remainder in a food processor with a tablespoon of cold water and the icing sugar. Blend to a purée, then pass through a sieve into a bowl. Set aside.

5 Place the egg yolks in a heatproof bowl and set over a pan of simmering water. Whisk the reduced wine mixture into the egg yolks and continue to whisk until the mixture is very light and just thick enough to leave a ribbon trail when the whisk is lifted. Remove from the heat and continue to whisk for 1 minute to stabilize the mixture. Fold in the raspberry purée.

6 Remove the pears from the pan and drain well on kitchen paper. Arrange upright on serving plates and spoon over the raspberry zabaglione. Decorate the pear stalks with a mint sprig and each plate with a small pile of the reserved raspberries. Add a light dusting of icing sugar to serve.

94 Strawberry Torte with Brandy and Chocolate Sauce

PHIL VICKERY'S DESSERT

Serves 2

200 ml/7 fl oz double cream, well chilled

50 g/2 oz caster sugar

115 g/4 oz mascarpone cheese, well chilled

finely grated rind of 1 lime

10 large strawberries, hulled and halved lengthways

6 fresh mint leaves

about 2 tsp brandy

FOR THE CHOCOLATE SAUCE:

50 g/2 oz cocoa powder

2 tbsp caster sugar

1 tbsp boiling water

This is a variation on one of my favourite desserts, which I cook at home when I have only half an hour to spare. I can promise you that no one will ever guess you haven't been slaving away for hours in the kitchen. It is important that the cream and mascarpone cheese are well chilled if you want to be able to serve the tortes immediately.

1 Place the cream and caster sugar in a large bowl and lightly whip until the mixture forms soft peaks. Fold in the mascarpone cheese and lime rind.

2 Place a 10 cm/4 in cooking ring on each of two serving plates and line with the strawberry halves, cut side against the ring. Spoon in the cream mixture and gently press to the edges, keeping the strawberries in place. Level off the tops of the tortes with a palette knife briefly dipped in boiling water. Chill for at least 5 minutes to set (up to 8 hours is fine if time allows).

3 Meanwhile, make the chocolate sauce. Place the cocoa powder and caster sugar in a small pan with the boiling water and simmer gently to combine, stirring occasionally. Remove from the heat and allow to cool.

4 Remove the cooking rings by carefully warming the edges with a blowtorch or warm cloth and then lifting them straight off. Arrange the mint leaves on top of each torte and drizzle over the brandy. Drizzle the chocolate sauce around the edges of the plates and serve at once.

95 Chocolate Drop Scones with Pecan Toffee Sauce

TONY TOBIN'S DESSERT

Serves 4

115 g/4 oz self-raising flour

¹⁄₄ tsp baking powder

2 eggs (preferably organic or free-range)

about 120 ml/4 fl oz milk

1 tbsp clear honey

50 g/2 oz plain chocolate, finely chopped (at least 70% cocoa solids)

FOR THE SAUCE:

50 g/2 oz caster sugar

50 g/2 oz pecan nuts, chopped

150 ml/¹⁄₄ pint double cream

vanilla ice cream, to serve (optional)

These rich, fluffy drop scones – little pancakes – are packed with flavour and the perfect way to round off a meal. They take minutes to prepare and even less time to devour. The secret is in the batter, which should be the consistency of thick cream and must be mixed as quickly and as lightly as possible.

1 To make the sauce, place the sugar in a heavy-based pan and cook over a low heat until dissolved and a caramel has formed. Do not be tempted to stir this or you'll end up with a pan of crystallized sugar. Add the pecan nuts, shaking the pan until the nuts are well coated in the caramel, then pour in the cream and cook gently until evenly dispersed and slightly thickened, swirling the pan occasionally. Keep warm.

2 Meanwhile, heat a non-stick flat griddle or frying pan. Sieve the flour into a bowl with the baking powder. Place the eggs in a jug with the milk, then lightly whisk to combine. Make a well in the centre of the flour and gradually add in enough of the egg mixture to make a smooth batter – the consistency of thick cream. Fold in the honey and chocolate.

3 Ladle spoonfuls of the batter on the heated pan, allowing them to spread out to about 7.5 cm/3 in in diameter. Reduce the heat and cook for about 1¹⁄₂ minutes until small bubbles appear on the surface. Turn over and cook for another 1–2 minutes until lightly golden. Stack on a plate and keep warm. Repeat until you have twelve drop scones in total. Arrange on warmed serving plates and spoon over the pecan toffee sauce. Add a scoop of ice cream, if liked, to serve.

96 Little Chocolate Chilli Pots

PAUL RANKIN'S DESSERT

Serves 2

4 egg yolks

55 g/2 oz caster sugar

1 vanilla pod

150 ml/¼ pint double cream

50 ml/2 fl oz milk

1 tsp ground cinnamon

1 tsp chilli powder

25 g/1 oz cocoa powder, plus extra for dusting

Over the years I've got to grips with the microwave on the *Ready Steady Cook* set as it allows me to achieve things in double-quick time. These little custard pots are a perfect example. Although they would be best cooked in a bain-marie (small roasting tin half-filled with boiling water) in a preheated oven at 150°C/300°F/Gas 2 (fan oven 130°C from cold) for about 25–30 minutes or until just set, I was able to make them from start to finish in less than ten. Just be careful if you cook them in the microwave not to overcook the mixture or the eggs will scramble, ruining the smooth, creamy texture.

1 Place the egg yolks and caster sugar in a bowl, then whisk until light and fluffy using an electric beater or by hand with a wooden spoon. Set aside.

2 Cut the vanilla pod in half with a sharp knife, then with a teaspoon scrape out the seeds and place in a pan (use the pod in another dish or to flavour sugar). Add the cream and milk to the pan, then whisk in the cinnamon, chilli and cocoa powder. Slowly bring to the boil, whisking continuously.

3 Gradually pour the cream mixture into the egg yolks and sugar, beating constantly to combine. Divide between two 120 ml/4 fl oz ramekins, cover with clingfilm and pierce the clingfilm a couple of times with the tip of a sharp knife. Cook in the microwave on high for 2 minutes, then leave to rest for 2 minutes before cooking on high again for 1 minute or until almost set, depending on the power of your machine.

4 Remove the ramekins from the microwave and allow to sit for 1 minute, then take off the clingfilm and dust with a little extra cocoa powder. Serve warm set on serving plates, or cold – they will keep happily in the fridge for up to 24 hours.

97 Chocolate Orange Cheesecakes

NICK NAIRN'S DESSERT

Serves 4

sunflower oil, for greasing

115 g/4 oz digestive biscuits, crushed

grated rind of 1 orange

½ tsp each mixed spice and ground cinnamon

50 g/2 oz unsalted butter, melted

225 g/8 oz plain chocolate

3 tbsp milk

3 tbsp brandy

225 g/8 oz full-fat soft cheese

150 ml/¼ pint double cream

1 tbsp caster sugar

cocoa powder, to dust

sugared needle shreds, to serve (optional – see introduction)

I like to serve these cheesecakes with sugared needle shreds, which are very easy to make. Simply pare the rind from an orange and cut into shreds. Heat 115 g/4 oz sugar in a pan with 50 ml/2 fl oz water until dissolved. Stir in the orange shreds and simmer for 10 minutes until completely tender, then drain, discarding the syrup. Spread the needle shreds on a plate and sprinkle with caster sugar. Leave to cool and set, then use to decorate as described below.

1 Lightly oil four 10 cm/4 in cooking moulds and place on an oiled baking sheet. Place the biscuits in a bowl and add the orange rind, mixed spice and cinnamon. Stir in the melted butter and divide the mixture between the four moulds, pressing down with the back of a spoon to form a base. Chill.

2 Melt the chocolate in a heatproof bowl set over a pan of simmering water. Transfer half into a separate bowl, set aside and allow to cool a little. To make the chocolate sauce, stir the milk and one tablespoon of the brandy into the remaining melted chocolate. Remove from the heat and leave to cool.

3 Place the cream cheese in a large bowl with the double cream, sugar and remaining two tablespoons of brandy. Combine with an electric beater until smooth and holding its shape, then fold in the cooled melted chocolate. Spoon on to the chilled biscuit bases and level with a palette knife that has been briefly dipped in water. Chill for at least 5 minutes (or up to 24 hours is fine).

4 Remove the cheesecakes from the fridge. Remove the moulds by warming the sides with a cloth that has been dipped in hot water and squeezed dry. Hold this around the sides of each mould for a few seconds before carefully lifting it off. Dust the cheesecakes with cocoa powder and arrange on serving plates. Decorate with sugared needle shreds, if liked, and pour around the chocolate sauce to serve.

98 Butternut Squash Sponges with Coconut Icing

ROSS BURDEN'S DESSERT

Serves 4

120 ml/4 fl oz olive oil, plus extra for brushing

$\frac{1}{2}$ small butternut squash (about 150 g/5 oz)

115 g/4 oz light muscovado sugar

2 eggs (preferably organic or free-range)

150 g/5 oz self-raising flour

$\frac{1}{2}$ tsp baking powder

$\frac{1}{2}$ tsp each ground cinnamon and ginger

150 g/5 oz icing sugar

about 2 tbsp coconut milk

These moist sponges would make a perfect tea-time treat, or they could be easily transported for a picnic. Spices do not last indefinitely in your cupboard and if they have been hanging around too long you might as well be using sawdust. Give them a good sniff: if they are not strongly scented, they have lost their taste, too.

1 Preheat the oven to 220°C/425°F/Gas 7 (fan oven 200°C from cold). Brush a four-holed Yorkshire pudding mould with a little oil. Peel the butternut squash and then grate using a mandolin or use a food processor with an attachment blade. Place the muscovado sugar and eggs in a large bowl and use an electric beater to whisk together until light and fluffy.

2 Sift the flour into a bowl with the baking powder and spices. Gradually whisk the oil into the egg mixture, adding the flour mixture tablespoon by tablespoon to prevent the mixture from curdling. Finally fold in the grated butternut squash and divide between the prepared Yorkshire pudding moulds. Bake for 10–12 minutes or until cooked through and lightly golden.

3 Meanwhile, sift the icing sugar into a small bowl and then beat in enough coconut milk to make a smooth icing. Remove the sponges from the oven and tip out of the moulds, then turn out on a wire rack and leave to cool a little. Drizzle the coconut icing over the sponges and arrange on serving plates.

99 Caramelized Panettone and Banana Pudding

ANTONY WORRALL
THOMPSON'S DESSERT

Serves 4

115 g/4 oz unsalted butter, plus extra for greasing

115 g/4 oz light muscovado sugar

4 tbsp golden syrup

4 firm ripe bananas

6 slices panettone

85 ml/3 fl oz double cream

85 ml/3 fl oz milk

thickened double cream or vanilla ice cream, to serve (optional)

I was so pleased with this recipe on the show that I called it my 'Sexy Toffee Pudding' and subsequently reproduced a version of it on *Food and Drink*. Serve it with thickened double cream if you dare, or vanilla ice cream for that cooling sensation. If you haven't got panettone, which is a sweet Italian Christmas bread, good quality raisin bread makes an excellent alternative.

1 Preheat the oven to 230°C/450°F/Gas 8 (fan oven 210°C from cold) and preheat the grill to very hot. Place the butter in a pan with the sugar and golden syrup and cook gently, stirring, until the butter and sugar have melted and the mixture has become a bubbling toffee sauce. Peel the bananas and cut into 2.5 cm/1 in slices, then add to the pan of toffee and simmer for 3–4 minutes, stirring occasionally.

2 Lightly butter a 1.7-litre/3-pint ovenproof dish and line with three of the panettone slices, cutting them as necessary to fit. Pour the cream into a small pan with the milk and heat gently, then pour half over the layer of panettone. Spoon half of the banana toffee mixture on top and cover with the rest of the panettone. Pour over the remaining cream mixture and cover with the rest of the banana toffee mixture. Bake for 10–12 minutes until heated through and just set, then quickly caramelize under the grill. Serve straight from the dish on to warmed serving plates with the cream or ice cream, if liked.

100 Apple Crisp with Orange-scented Custard

BRIAN TURNER'S DESSERT

Serves 2

40 g/1½ oz unsalted butter, plus extra for greasing

2 Granny Smith apples, peeled, cored and sliced

2 tbsp dark muscovado sugar

¼ tsp ground cinnamon

2 tbsp sultanas

150 g/5 oz fresh white breadcrumbs

4 tsp clear honey

200 ml/7 fl oz double cream

2 egg yolks

2 tbsp caster sugar

1 tsp finely grated orange rind

1 fresh rosemary sprig

icing sugar, for dusting

Nothing can beat a classic British pudding on a cold winter's day. Puddings are so much a part of our heritage that it is not surprising they are fast becoming fashionable again. This is a speedy variation on the traditional apple brown betty, which I still occasionally have on the menu in my restaurant. I am serving it here with an orange-scented custard, which cuts the richness of the pudding perfectly.

1 Preheat the oven to 220°C/425°F/Gas 7 (fan oven 200°C from cold). Heat a sauté pan and melt half the butter. Add the apples, tossing to coat, then sprinkle over the sugar and cinnamon. Cook for 2–3 minutes until the apples are lightly caramelized but still holding their shape. Stir in the sultanas and divide half the mixture between two lightly buttered individual ovenproof dishes. Place the remainder in a bowl and set aside.

2 In the same pan, melt the remaining butter and fry the breadcrumbs until crisp and golden. Sprinkle half over the top of the apple mixture in the dishes. Spread over the remaining apple mixture and then sprinkle over the rest of the breadcrumbs to cover the top completely. Drizzle with the honey and bake for 8–10 minutes or until bubbling and lightly golden.

3 Meanwhile, make the orange-scented custard. Gently warm the cream in a small pan. Place the egg yolks and sugar in a bowl and whisk to combine. Gently pour in the heated cream, whisking continuously. Pour the mixture into a clean pan and stir in the orange rind and rosemary sprig, then cook over a low heat until thickened, stirring with a wooden spoon. Remove from the heat, discard the rosemary sprig and pour into a serving jug. Set the apple crisps on heatproof serving plates, add a light dusting of icing sugar and serve with the jug of orange-scented custard.

Index

Page numbers in *italics* refer to illustrations